React Native Blueprint

Create eight exciting native cross-platform mobile applications with JavaScript

Emilio Rodriguez Martinez

BIRMINGHAM - MUMBAI

React Native Blueprints

First published: November 2017

Production reference: 1061117

Published by Packt Publishing Ltd.
Livery Place
35 Livery Street
Birmingham
B3 2PB, UK.
ISBN 978-1-78728-809-6

www.packtpub.com

Credits

Author
Emilio Rodriguez Martinez

Reviewers
Mike Grabowski
Christoph Michel
Alessandro Molina

Acquisition Editor
Reshma Raman

Content Development Editor
Jason Pereira

Technical Editor
Prajakta Mhatre

Copy Editor
Charlotte Carneiro

Project Coordinator
Sheejal Shah

Proofreader
Safis Editing

Indexer
Rekha Nair

Production Coordinator
Melwyn D'sa

About the Author

Emilio Rodriguez Martinez is a senior software engineer who has been working on highly demanding JavaScript projects since 2010. He transitioned from web development positions into mobile development, first with hybrid technologies such as Cordova and then with native JavaScript solutions such as Titanium.

In 2015, he focused on the development and maintenance of several apps built in React Native, some of which were featured in Apple's App Store as the top apps of the week. Nowadays, Emilio is part of the Red Hat mobile team, which leverages Red Hat's open source mobile platform. He serves as an advocate for mobile developers using RHMAP. He is also an active contributor to React Native's codebase and StackOverflow, where he provides advice on React and React Native questions.

About the Reviewers

Mike Grabowski is a CTO and co-founder of Callstack (`callstack.com`), a consultancy that helps developers and businesses launch their apps for everyone, on many platforms, at the same time. Right now, it is done with the help of React Native. He is also on a React Native core team where he helps to orchestrate monthly releases of the framework. At Callstack, he does a whole bunch of open source activities for the community, including React Native EU--the first conference to focus on React Native in the world. When not working, he enjoys driving his BMW on a race track.

Christoph Michel is a software engineer who's been involved with React Native since its early release in 2015. He has published several React Native apps on the App Store. He also develops open source components and writes technical articles on `cmichel.io`.

Alessandro Molina, partner at AXANT.it, a software engineer at Crunch.IO, and a father of two, has been passionate about web and mobile development for the past 15 years. He is particularly involved in the Python community and is the author of the DukPy project, which runs React and JavaScript in pure Python environments. He is also a core developer of the TurboGears2 Python Web Framework and co-maintainer of widely used web development libraries and technologies in Python and MongoDB environments such as the Beaker Session and Caching framework and the Ming MongoDB ODM.

He was also the original author of the AXMEAS hybrid multiplatform mobile development framework, which is used to create mobile apps that run on iOS, Android, Windows, and on other browsers. In his spare time, Alessandro enjoys exploring big data and machine learning solutions applied to nearly real-time use cases and traveling with his family to learn new things, not only about software but about the world and culture too.

www.PacktPub.com

For support files and downloads related to your book, please visit www.PacktPub.com. Did you know that Packt offers eBook versions of every book published, with PDF and ePub files available? You can upgrade to the eBook version at www.PacktPub.com and as a print book customer, you are entitled to a discount on the eBook copy. Get in touch with us at service@packtpub.com for more details.

At www.PacktPub.com, you can also read a collection of free technical articles, sign up for a range of free newsletters and receive exclusive discounts and offers on Packt books and eBooks.

https://www.packtpub.com/mapt

Get the most in-demand software skills with Mapt. Mapt gives you full access to all Packt books and video courses, as well as industry-leading tools to help you plan your personal development and advance your career.

Why subscribe?

- Fully searchable across every book published by Packt
- Copy and paste, print, and bookmark content
- On demand and accessible via a web browser

Customer Feedback

Thanks for purchasing this Packt book. At Packt, quality is at the heart of our editorial process. To help us improve, please leave us an honest review on this book's Amazon page at https://www.amazon.com/dp/1787288099.

If you'd like to join our team of regular reviewers, you can e-mail us at customerreviews@packtpub.com. We award our regular reviewers with free eBooks and videos in exchange for their valuable feedback. Help us be relentless in improving our products!

Table of Contents

Preface

React Native helps web and mobile developers to build apps for iOS and Android apps that perform at the same level as any other natively developed app. The range of apps that can be built using this library is huge. From e-commerce to games, React Native is a good fit for any mobile project due to its flexibility and extendable nature. It has good performance, reuses React knowledge, has the ability to import npm packages, and uses the same codebase for iOS and Android. There's no doubt React Native is not only a good alternative to native development, but also a great way to introduce web developers to a mobile project. This book aims to give JavaScript and React developers a peek at how some of the most popular apps in the market could be built from scratch with React Native. We will build all the apps in iOS and Android, except for those cases where the apps only make sense on one of the platforms.

What this book covers

Chapter 1, *Shopping List,* shows how a groceries list can be built in React Native using simple navigation and introducing some of the most common native components.

Chapter 2, *RSS Reader,* teaches you how to create a news feed reader using RSS.

Chapter 3, *Car Booking App,* explains how some of the most popular car-sharing apps could have been developed using React Native.

Chapter 4, *Image Sharing App,* teaches you the fundamentals of how a social network based on image sharing can be created with React Native.

Chapter 5, *Guitar Tuner,* is one of the apps that require components not yet available in React Native. We will build one of these native components and use it from a React Native app.

Chapter 6, *Messaging App,* 1:1 messaging apps are the most popular apps in the stores. In this chapter, we will build a full-featured messaging app including push notifications and cloud-based storage.

Chapter 7, *Game,* is fun and shows you the fundamentals of how a 2D game can be developed using React Native.

Chapter 8, *E-Commerce App,* uses React Native to build one of the most requested types of app in the market: an e-commerce app to buy and sell products online.

What you need for this book

Most of the apps built throughout this book will run on Android and iOS, so a computer running Linux, Windows, or OSX will be required, although we recommend any Apple computer (running OSX 10 or later) to run both mobile platforms at once, as some examples will require working on XCode, which is only installable on OSX.

Other pieces of software we will use in examples are:

- XCode
- Android Studio
- A React-ready IDE (such as Atom, VS Code, and SublimeText)

And of course, we will need React Native and React Native CLI installed (`https://facebook.github.io/react-native/docs/getting-started.html`).

Who this book is for

This book is targeted at JavaScript developers trying to understand how different kinds of apps can be built using React Native. They will find a set of best practices and proven architectural strategies that can be applied to building any kind of app.

Although some basic concepts of React won't be explained in this book, no specific React skills are needed to follow along, since we won't dive deep into complex React patterns.

Conventions

In this book, you will find a number of text styles that distinguish between different kinds of information. Here are some examples of these styles and an explanation of their meaning.

Code words in text, database table names, folder names, filenames, file extensions, pathnames, dummy URLs, user input, and Twitter handles are shown as follows: "We have to create an `src` folder where we will store all our React code."

Also in big code blocks, when some pieces of code are not relevant or reviewed in a different place, they will be replaced by an ellipsis (...).

A block of code is set as follows:

```
/*** index.js ***/

import { AppRegistry } from 'react-native';
import App from './src/main';
AppRegistry.registerComponent('GroceriesList', () => App);
```

Any command-line input or output is written as follows:

```
react-native run-ios
```

New terms and **important words** are shown in bold. Words that you see on the screen, for example, in menus or dialog boxes, appear in the text like this: "The back button on the **Add a product** screen."

Tips and important notes appear in a box like this.

Tips and tricks appear like this.

Reader feedback

Feedback from our readers is always welcome. Let us know what you think about this book--what you liked or disliked. Reader feedback is important to us as it helps us develop titles that you will really get the most out of. To send us general feedback, simply email feedback@packtpub.com, and mention the book's title in the subject of your message. If there is a topic that you have expertise in and you are interested in either writing or contributing to a book, see our author guide at www.packtpub.com/authors.

Customer support

Now that you are the proud owner of a Packt book, we have a number of things to help you to get the most from your purchase.

Downloading the example code

You can download the example code files for this book from your account at
`http://www.packtpub.com`. If you purchased this book elsewhere, you can visit
`http://www.packtpub.com/support` and register to have the files e-mailed directly to you.
You can download the code files by following these steps:

1. Log in or register to our website using your e-mail address and password.
2. Hover the mouse pointer on the **SUPPORT** tab at the top.
3. Click on **Code Downloads & Errata**.
4. Enter the name of the book in the **Search** box.
5. Select the book for which you're looking to download the code files
6. Choose from the drop-down menu where you purchased this book from.
7. Click on **Code Download**.

Once the file is downloaded, please make sure that you unzip or extract the folder using the
latest version of:

- WinRAR / 7-Zip for Windows
- Zipeg / iZip / UnRarX for Mac
- 7-Zip / PeaZip for Linux

The code bundle for the book is also hosted on GitHub at `https://github.com/`
`PacktPublishing/React-Native-Blueprints`. We also have other code bundles from our
rich catalog of books and videos available at `https://github.com/PacktPublishing/`.
Check them out!

Downloading the color images of this book

We also provide you with a PDF file that has color images of the screenshots/diagrams used
in this book. The color images will help you better understand the changes in the output.
You can download this file from `https://www.packtpub.com/sites/default/files/`
`downloads/ReactNativeBlueprints_ColorImages.pdf`.

Errata

Although we have taken every care to ensure the accuracy of our content, mistakes do happen. If you find a mistake in one of our books-maybe a mistake in the text or the code-- we would be grateful if you could report this to us. By doing so, you can save other readers from frustration and help us improve subsequent versions of this book. If you find any errata, please report them by visiting http://www.packtpub.com/submit-errata, selecting your book, clicking on the **Errata Submission Form** link, and entering the details of your errata. Once your errata are verified, your submission will be accepted and the errata will be uploaded to our website or added to any list of existing errata under the Errata section of that title.

To view the previously submitted errata, go to https://www.packtpub.com/books/content/support and enter the name of the book in the search field. The required information will appear under the **Errata** section.

Piracy

Piracy of copyrighted material on the Internet is an ongoing problem across all media. At Packt, we take the protection of our copyright and licenses very seriously. If you come across any illegal copies of our works in any form on the internet, please provide us with the location address or website name immediately so that we can pursue a remedy.

Please contact us at copyright@packtpub.com with a link to the suspected pirated material.

We appreciate your help in protecting our authors and our ability to bring you valuable content.

Questions

If you have a problem with any aspect of this book, you can contact us at questions@packtpub.com, and we will do our best to address the problem.

1
Shopping List

Most of the modern languages and frameworks used to present a to-do list as their sample app. It is a great way to understand the basics of a framework as user interaction, basic navigation, or how to structure code. We'll start in a more pragmatic way: building a shopping list app.

You will be able to develop this app in React Native code, build it for both iOS and Android, and finally install it on your phone. This way, you could not only show your friends what you built, but also understand missing features that you can build by yourself, thinking about user-interface improvements, and above all, motivating yourself to keep learning React Native as you feel its true potential.

By the end of this chapter, you will have built a fully-functional shopping list that you can use on your phone and will have all the tools you need to create and maintain simple stateful apps.

Overview

One of the most powerful features of React Native is its cross-platform capabilities; we will build our shopping list app for both iOS and Android, reusing 99% of our code. Let's take a look at how the app will look on both platforms:

iOS:

After adding more products, this is how it will look:

Android:

After adding more products, this is how it will look:

The app will have a very similar user interface on both platforms, but we won't need to care much about the differences (for example, the back button on the **Add a product** screen), as they will be handled automatically by React Native.

It is important to understand that each platform has its own user interface patterns, and it's a good practice to follow them. For example, navigation is usually handled through tabs in iOS while Android prefers a drawer menu, so we should build both navigation patterns if we want happy users on both platforms. In any case, this is only a recommendation, and any user interface pattern could be built on every platform. In later chapters, we will see how to handle two different patterns in the most effective way within the same codebase.

The app comprises of two screens: your shopping list and a list of the products which could be added to your shopping list. The user can navigate from the **Shopping List** screen to the **Add a product** screen through the round blue button and back through the < **Back** button. We will also build a clear button in the shopping list screen (the round red button) and the ability to add and remove products on the **Add a product** screen.

We will be covering the following topics in this chapter:

- Folder structure for a basic React Native project
- React Native's basic CLI commands
- Basic navigation
- JS debugging
- Live reloading
- Styling with NativeBase
- Lists
- Basic state management
- Handling events
- `AsyncStorage`
- Prompt popups
- Distributing the app

Setting up our project

React Native has a very powerful CLI that we will need to install to get started with our project. To install, just run the following command in your command line (you might need to run this with `sudo`), if you don't have enough permissions:

```
npm install -g react-native-cli
```

Once the installation is finished, we can start using the React Native CLI by typing `react-native`. To start our project, we will run the following command:

```
react-native init --version="0.49.3" GroceriesList
```

This command will create a basic project named `GroceriesList` with all the dependencies and libraries you need to build the app on iOS and Android. Once the CLI has finished installing all the packages, you should have a folder structure similar to this:

The entry file for our project is `index.js`. If you want to see your initial app running on a simulator, you can use React Native's CLI again:

```
react-native run-ios
```

Or

```
react-native run-android
```

Provided you have XCode or Android Studio and Android Simulator installed, you should be able to see a sample screen on your simulator after compilation:

We have everything we need to set up to start implementing our app, but in order to easily debug and see our changes in the simulator, we need to enable two more features: remote JS debugging and live reloading.

For debugging, we will use *React Native Debugger*, a standalone app, based on the official debugger for React Native, which includes React Inspector and Redux DevTools. It can be downloaded following the instructions on its GitHub repository (`https://github.com/ jhen0409/react-native-debugger`). For this debugger to work properly, we will need to enable **Remote JS Debugging** from within our app by opening a React Native development menu within the simulator by pressing *command + ctrl + Z* on iOS or *command + M* on Android.

If everything goes well, we should see the following menu appear:

Now, we will press two buttons: **Debug Remote JS** and **Enable Live Reload**. Once we are done with this, we have all our development environment up and ready to start writing React code.

Setting up the folder structure

Our app only comprises of two screens: **Shopping List** and **Add Products**. Since the state for such a simple app should be easy to manage, we won't add any library for state management (for example, Redux), as we will send the shared state through the navigation component. This should make our folder structure rather simple:

We have to create an `src` folder where we will store all our React code. The self-created file `index.js` will have the following code:

```
/*** index.js ***/

import { AppRegistry } from 'react-native';
import App from './src/main';
AppRegistry.registerComponent('GroceriesList', () => App);
```

In short, these files will import the common root code for our app, store it in a variable named `App` and later pass this variable to the `AppRegistry` through the `registerComponent` method. `AppRegistry` is the component to which we should register our root components. Once we do this, React Native will generate a JS bundle for our app and then run the app when it's ready by invoking `AppRegistry.runApplication`.

Most of the code we will be writing, will be placed inside the `src` folder. For this app, we will create our root component (`main.js`) in this folder, and a `screens` subfolder, in which we will store our two screens (`ShoppingList` and `AddProduct`).

Now let's install all the initial dependencies for our app before continue coding. In our project's root folder, we will need to run the following command:

```
npm install
```

Running that command will install all the basic dependencies for every React Native project. Let's now install the three packages we will be using for this specific app:

```
npm install native-base --save
npm install react-native-prompt-android --save
npm install react-navigation --save
```

Further ahead in this chapter, we will explain what each package will be used for.

Adding a Navigation component

Most mobile apps comprise of more than one screen, so we will need to be able to "travel" between those screens. In order to achieve this, we will need a `Navigation` component. React Native comes with a `Navigator` and a `NavigatorIOS` component out of the box, although the React maintainers recommend using an external navigation solution built by the community named `react-navigation` (`https://github.com/react-community/react-navigation`), which is very performant, well maintained, and rich in features, so we will use it for our app.

Because we already installed our module for navigation (`react-navigation`), we can set up and initialize our `Navigation` component inside our `main.js` file:

```
/*** src/main.js ***/

import React from 'react';
import { StackNavigator } from 'react-navigation';
import ShoppingList from './screens/ShoppingList.js';
import AddProduct from './screens/AddProduct.js';

const Navigator = StackNavigator({
  ShoppingList: { screen: ShoppingList },
  AddProduct: { screen: AddProduct }
});

export default class App extends React.Component {
  constructor() {
    super();
  }

  render() {
    return <Navigator />;
  }
}
```

Our root component imports both of the screens in our app (`ShoppingList` and `AddProduct`) and passes them to the `StackNavigator` function, which generates the `Navigator` component. Let's take a deeper look into how `StackNavigator` works.

`StackNavigator` provides a way for any app to transition between screens, where each new screen is placed on top of a stack. When we request the navigation to a new screen, `StackNavigator` will slide the new screen from the right and place a `<` `Back` button in the upper-right corner to go back to the previous screen in iOS or, will fade in from the bottom while a new screen is placing a `<-` arrow to go back in Android. With the same codebase, we will trigger familiar navigation patterns in iOS and Android. `StackNavigator` is also really simple to use, as we only need to pass the screens in our apps as a hash map, where the keys are the names we want for our screens and the values are the imported screens as React components. The result is a `<Navigator/>` component which we can render to initialize our app.

Styling our app with NativeBase

React Native includes a powerful way to style our components and screens using Flexbox and a CSS-like API but, for this app, we want to focus on the functionality aspect, so we will use a library including basic styled components as buttons, lists, icons, menus, forms, and many more. It can be seen as a Twitter Bootstrap for React Native.

There are several popular UI libraries, NativeBase and React Native elements being the two most popular and best supported. Out of these two, we will choose NativeBase, since it's documentation is slightly clearer for beginners.

You can find the detailed documentation on how NativeBase works on their website (`https://docs.nativebase.io/`), but we will go through the basics of installing and using some of their components in this chapter. We previously installed `native-base` as a dependency of our project through `npm install` but NativeBase includes some peer dependencies, which need to be linked and included in our iOS and Android native folders. Luckily, React Native already has a tool for finding out those dependencies and linking them; we just need to run:

```
react-native link
```

At this point, we have all the UI components from NativeBase fully available in our app. So, we can start building our first screen.

Building the ShoppingList screen

Our first screen will contain a list of the items we need to buy, so it will contain one list item per item we need to buy, including a button to mark that item as already bought. Moreover, we need a button to navigate to the `AddProduct` screen, which will allow us to add products to our list. Finally, we will add a button to clear the list of products, in case we want to start a new shopping list:

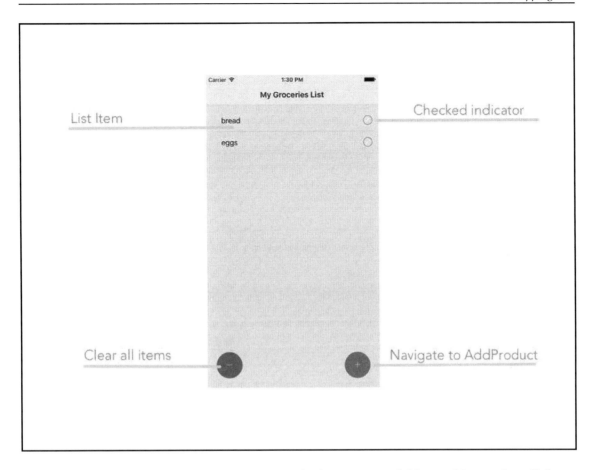

Let's start by creating `ShoppingList.js` inside the `screens` folder and importing all the UI components we will need from `native-base` and `react-native` (we will use an alert popup to warn the user before clearing all items). The main UI components we will be using are `Fab` (the blue and red round buttons), `List`, `ListItem`, `CheckBox`, `Text`, and `Icon`. To support our layout, we will be using `Body`, `Container`, `Content`, and `Right`, which are layout containers for the rest of our components.

Having all these components, we can create a simple version of our `ShoppingList` component:

```
/*** ShoppingList.js ***/
import React from 'react';
import { Alert } from 'react-native';
import {
  Body,
  Container,
```

```
    Content,
    Right,
    Text,
    CheckBox,
    List,
    ListItem,
    Fab,
    Icon
} from 'native-base';

export default class ShoppingList extends React.Component {
  static navigationOptions = {
    title: 'My Groceries List'
  };
  /*** Render ***/
  render() {
    return (
      <Container>
        <Content>
          <List>
            <ListItem>
              <Body>
                <Text>'Name of the product'</Text>
              </Body>
              <Right>
                <CheckBox
                  checked={false}
                />
              </Right>
            </ListItem>
          </List>
        </Content>
        <Fab
          style={{ backgroundColor: '#5067FF' }}
          position="bottomRight"
        >
          <Icon name="add" />
        </Fab>
        <Fab
          style={{ backgroundColor: 'red' }}
          position="bottomLeft"
        >
          <Icon ios="ios-remove" android="md-remove" />
        </Fab>
      </Container>
    );
  }
}
```

This is just a dumb component statically displaying the components we will be using on this screen. Some things to note:

- `navigationOptions` is a static attribute which will be used by `<Navigator>` to configure how the navigation would behave. In our case, we want to display **My Groceries List** as the title for this screen.
- For `native-base` to do its magic, we need to use `<Container>` and `<Content>` to properly form the layout.
- `Fab` buttons are placed outside `<Content>`, so they can float over the left and right-bottom corners.
- Each `ListItem` contains a `<Body>` (main text) and a `<Right>` (icons aligned to the right).

Since we enabled **Live Reload** in our first steps, we should see the app reloading after saving our newly created file. All the UI elements are now in place, but they are not functional since we didn't add any state. This should be our next step.

Adding state to our screen

Let's add some initial state to our `ShoppingList` screen to populate the list with actual dynamic data. We will start by creating a constructor and setting the initial state there:

```
/*** ShoppingList.js ***/

...
constructor(props) {
  super(props);
  this.state = {
    products: [{ id: 1, name: 'bread' }, { id: 2, name: 'eggs' }]
  };
}
...
```

Now, we can render that state inside of `<List>` (inside the `render` method):

```
/*** ShoppingList.js ***/

...
<List>
  {
    this.state.products.map(p => {
      return (
        <ListItem
```

```
            key={p.id}
        >
          <Body>
            <Text style={{ color: p.gotten ? '#bbb' : '#000' }}>
              {p.name}
            </Text>
          </Body>
          <Right>
            <CheckBox
              checked={p.gotten}
            />
          </Right>
        </ListItem>
      );
    }
  )}
</List>
...
```

We now rely on a list of products inside our component's state, each product storing an `id`, a `name`, and `gotten` properties. When modifying this state, we will automatically be re-rendering the list.

Now, it's time to add some event handlers, so we can modify the state at the users' command or navigate to the `AddProduct` screen.

Adding event handlers

All the interaction with the user will happen through event handlers in React Native. Depending on the controller, we will have different events which can be triggered. The most common event is `onPress`, as it will be triggered every time we push a button, a checkbox, or a view in general. Let's add some `onPress` handlers for all the components which can be pushed in our screen:

```
/*** ShoppingList.js ***/

...
render() {
 return (
   <Container>
     <Content>
       <List>
         {this.state.products.map(p => {
           return (
             <ListItem
```

```
            key={p.id}
            onPress={this._handleProductPress.bind(this, p)}
         >
            <Body>
              <Text style={{ color: p.gotten ? '#bbb' : '#000' }}>
                {p.name}
              </Text>
            </Body>
            <Right>
              <CheckBox
                checked={p.gotten}
                onPress={this._handleProductPress.bind(this, p)}
              />
            </Right>
          </ListItem>
        );
      })}
      </List>
    </Content>
    <Fab
      style={{ backgroundColor: '#5067FF' }}
      position="bottomRight"
      onPress={this._handleAddProductPress.bind(this)}
    >
      <Icon name="add" />
    </Fab>
    <Fab
      style={{ backgroundColor: 'red' }}
      position="bottomLeft"
      onPress={this._handleClearPress.bind(this)}
    >
      <Icon ios="ios-remove" android="md-remove" />
    </Fab>
  </Container>
  );
}
...
```

Notice we added three onPress event handlers:

- On <ListItem>, to react when the user taps on one product in the list
- On <CheckBox>, to react when the user taps on the checkbox icon next to every product in the list
- On both the <Fab> buttons

If you know React, you probably understand why we use `.bind` in all our handler functions, but, in case you have doubts, `.bind` will make sure we can use `this` inside the definition of our handlers as a reference to the component itself instead of the global scope. This will allow us to call methods inside our components as `this.setState` or read our component's attributes, such as `this.props` and `this.state`.

For the cases when the user taps on a specific product, we also bind the product itself, so we can use them inside our event handlers.

Now, let's define the functions which will serve as event handlers:

```
/*** ShoppingList.js ***/

. . .
_handleProductPress(product) {
 this.state.products.forEach(p => {
   if (product.id === p.id) {
     p.gotten = !p.gotten;
   }
   return p;
 });

 this.setState({ products: this.state.products });
}
. . .
```

First, let's create a handler for when the user taps on a product from our shopping list or in its checkbox. We want to mark the product as `gotten` (or unmark it if it was already `gotten`), so we will update the state with the product marked properly.

Next, we will add a handler for the blue `<Fab>` button to navigate to the `AddProduct` screen:

```
/*** ShoppingList.js ***/

. . .
_handleAddProductPress() {
  this.props.navigation.navigate('AddProduct', {
    addProduct: product => {
      this.setState({
        products: this.state.products.concat(product)
      });
    },
    deleteProduct: product => {
      this.setState({
        products: this.state.products.filter(p => p.id !== product.id)
```

```
        });
      },
      productsInList: this.state.products
    });
  }
  ...
```

This handler uses `this.props.navigation`, which is a property automatically passed by the `Navigator` component from `react-navigation`. This property contains a method named `navigate`, receiving the name of the screen to which the app should navigate plus an object which can be used as a global state. In the case of this app, we will store three keys:

- `addProduct`: One function to allow the `AddProduct` screen to modify the `ShoppingList` component's state to reflect the action of adding a new product to the shopping list.
- `deleteProduct`: One function to allow the `AddProduct` screen to modify the `ShoppingList` component's state to reflect the action of removing a product from the shopping list.
- `productsInList`: A variable holding the list of products is already on the shopping list, so the `AddProducts` screen can know which products were already added to the shopping list and display those as "already added", preventing the addition of duplicate items.

Handling state within the navigation should be seen as a workaround for simple apps containing a limited number of screens. In larger apps (as we will see in later chapters), a state management library, such as Redux or MobX, should be used to keep the separation between pure data and user interface handling.

We will add the last handler for the blue `<Fab>` button, which enables the user to clear all the items in the shopping list in case you want to start a new list:

```
/*** ShoppingList.js ***/

...
_handleClearPress() {
  Alert.alert('Clear all items?', null, [
    { text: 'Cancel' },
    { text: 'Ok', onPress: () => this.setState({ products: [] }) }
  ]);
}
...
```

We are using `Alert` to prompt the user for confirmation before clearing all the elements in our shopping list. Once the user confirms this action, we will empty the `products` attribute in our component's state.

Putting it all together

Let's see how the whole component's structure would look like when putting all the methods together:

```
/*** ShoppingList.js ***/

import React from 'react';
import { Alert } from 'react-native';
import { ... } from 'native-base';

export default class ShoppingList extends React.Component {
 static navigationOptions = {
   title: 'My Groceries List'
 };

 constructor(props) {
   ...
 }

 /*** User Actions Handlers ***/
 _handleProductPress(product) {
   ...
 }

 _handleAddProductPress() {
   ...
 }

 _handleClearPress() {
   ...
 }

 /*** Render ***/
 render() {
   ...
 }
}
```

The structure of a React Native component is very similar to a normal React component. We need to import React itself and then some components to build up our screen. We also have several event handlers (which we have prefixed with an underscore as a mere convention) and finally a `render` method to display our components using standard JSX.

The only difference with a React web app is the fact that we are using React Native UI components instead of DOM components.

Building the AddProduct screen

As the user will have the need of adding new products to the shopping list, we need to build a screen in which we can prompt the user for the name of the product to be added and save it in the phone's storage for later use.

Using AsyncStorage

When building a React Native app, it's important to understand how mobile devices handle the memory used by each app. Our app will be sharing the memory with the rest of the apps in the device so, eventually, the memory which is using our app will be claimed by a different app. Therefore, we cannot rely on putting data in memory for later use. In case we want to make sure the data is available across users of our app, we need to store that data in the device's persistent storage.

React Native offers an API to handle the communication with the persistent storage in our mobile devices and this API is the same on iOS and Android, so we can write cross-platform code comfortably.

The API is named `AsyncStorage`, and we can use it after importing from React Native:

```
import { AsyncStorage } from 'react-native';
```

We will only use two methods from `AsyncStorage`: `getItem` and `setItem`. For example, we will create within our screen a local function to handle the addition of a product to the full list of products:

```
/*** AddProduct ***/

...
async addNewProduct(name) {
  const newProductsList = this.state.allProducts.concat({
    name: name,
    id: Math.floor(Math.random() * 100000)
```

```
  });

  await AsyncStorage.setItem(
    '@allProducts',
    JSON.stringify(newProductsList)
  );

  this.setState({
    allProducts: newProductsList
  });
}
...
```

There are some interesting things to note here:

- We are using ES7 features such as `async` and `await` to handle asynchronous calls instead of promises or callbacks. Understanding ES7 is outside the scope of this book, but it is recommended to learn and understand about the use of `async` and `await`, as it's a very powerful feature we will be using extensively throughout this book.
- Every time we add a product to `allProducts`, we also call `AsyncStorage.setItem` to permanently store the product in our device's storage. This action ensures that the products added by the user will be available even when the operating system clears the memory used by our app.
- We need to pass two parameters to `setItem` (and also to `getItem`): a key and a value. Both of them must be strings, so we would need to use `JSON.stringify`, if we want to store the JSON-formatted data.

Adding state to our screen

As we have just seen, we will be using an attribute in our component's state named `allProducts`, which will contain the full list of products the user can add to the shopping list.

We can initialize this state inside the component's constructor to give the user a gist of what he/she will be seeing on this screen even during the first run of the app (this is a trick used by many modern apps to onboard users by faking a `used` state):

```
/*** AddProduct.js ***/

...
constructor(props) {
  super(props);
```

```
      this.state = {
        allProducts: [
          { id: 1, name: 'bread' },
          { id: 2, name: 'eggs' },
          { id: 3, name: 'paper towels' },
          { id: 4, name: 'milk' }
        ],
        productsInList: []
      };
  }
  ...
```

Besides allProducts, we will also have a productsInList array, holding all the products which are already added to the current shopping list. This will allow us to mark the product as Already in shopping list, preventing the user from trying to add the same product twice in the list.

This constructor will be very useful for our app's first run but once the user has added products (and therefore saved them in persistent storage), we want those products to display instead of this test data. In order to achieve this functionality, we should read the saved products from AsyncStorage and set it as the initial allProducts value in our state. We will do this on componentWillMount:

```
/*** AddProduct.js ***/

...
async componentWillMount() {
  const savedProducts = await AsyncStorage.getItem('@allProducts');
  if(savedProducts) {
    this.setState({
      allProducts: JSON.parse(savedProducts)
    });
  }

  this.setState({
    productsInList: this.props.navigation.state.params.productsInList
  });
}
...
```

We are updating the state once the screen is ready to be mounted. First, we will update the allProducts value by reading it from the persistent storage. Then, we will update the list productsInList based on what the ShoppingList screen has set as the state in the navigation property.

With this state, we can build our list of products, which can be added to the shopping list:

```
/*** AddProduct ***/

...
render(){
  <List>
    {this.state.allProducts.map(product => {
      const productIsInList = this.state.productsInList.find(
        p => p.id === product.id
      );
      return (
        <ListItem key={product.id}>
          <Body>
            <Text
              style={{
                color: productIsInList ? '#bbb' : '#000'
              }}
            >
              {product.name}
            </Text>
            {
              productIsInList &&
              <Text note>
                {'Already in shopping list'}
              </Text>
            }
          </Body>
        </ListItem>
      );
    }
  )}
  </List>
}
...
```

Inside our `render` method, we will use an `Array.map` function to iterate and print each possible product, checking if the product is already added to the current shopping list to display a note, warning the user: `Already in shopping list`.

Of course, we still need to add a better layout, buttons, and event handlers for all the possible user actions. Let's start improving our `render` method to put all the functionality in place.

Adding event listeners

As it happened with the `ShoppingList` screen, we want the user to be able to interact with our `AddProduct` component, so we will add some event handlers to respond to some user actions.

Our `render` method should then look something like this:

```
/*** AddProduct.js ***/

...
render() {
  return (
    <Container>
      <Content>
        <List>
          {this.state.allProducts.map(product => {
            const productIsInList = this.state.productsInList.
            find(p => p.id === product.id);
            return (
              <ListItem
                key={product.id}
                onPress={this._handleProductPress.bind
                (this, product)}
              >
                <Body>
                  <Text
                    style={{ color: productIsInList? '#bbb' : '#000' }}
                  >
                    {product.name}
                  </Text>
                  {
                    productIsInList &&
                    <Text note>
                      {'Already in shopping list'}
                    </Text>
                  }
                </Body>
                <Right>
                  <Icon
                    ios="ios-remove-circle"
                    android="md-remove-circle"
                    style={{ color: 'red' }}
                    onPress={this._handleRemovePress.bind(this,
                    product )}
                  />
                </Right>
```

```
                    </ListItem>
                );
              })}
            </List>
          </Content>
        <Fab
          style={{ backgroundColor: '#5067FF' }}
          position="bottomRight"
          onPress={this._handleAddProductPress.bind(this)}
        >
          <Icon name="add" />
        </Fab>
      </Container>
      );
  }
  ...
```

There are three event handlers responding to the three press events in this component:

- On the blue <Fab> button, which is in charge of adding new products to the products list
- On each <ListItem>, which will add the product to the shopping list
- On the delete icons inside each <ListItem> to remove this product from the list of the products, which can be added to the shopping list

Let's start adding new products to the available products list once the user presses the <Fab> button:

```
/*** AddProduct.js ***/

...
_handleAddProductPress() {
  prompt(
    'Enter product name',
    '',
    [
      { text: 'Cancel', style: 'cancel' },
      { text: 'OK', onPress: this.addNewProduct.bind(this) }
    ],
    {
      type: 'plain-text'
    }
  );
}
...
```

We are using here the `prompt` function from the `react-native-prompt-android` module. Despite its name, it's a cross-platform prompt-on-a-pop-up library, which we will use to add products through the `addNewProduct` function we created before. We need to import the `prompt` function before we use it, as follows:

```
import prompt from 'react-native-prompt-android';
```

And here is the output:

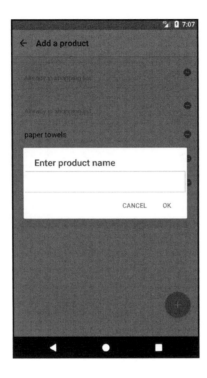

Once the user enters the name of the product and presses **OK**, the product will be added to the list so that we can move to the next event handler, adding products to the shopping list when the user taps on the product name:

```
/*** AddProduct.js ***/

...
_handleProductPress(product) {
  const productIndex = this.state.productsInList.findIndex(
    p => p.id === product.id
  );
  if (productIndex > -1) {
    this.setState({
      productsInList: this.state.productsInList.filter(
        p => p.id !== product.id
      )
    });
    this.props.navigation.state.params.deleteProduct(product);
  } else {
    this.setState({
      productsInList: this.state.productsInList.concat(product)
    });
```

```
        this.props.navigation.state.params.addProduct(product);
    }
  }
  ...
```

This handler checks if the selected product is on the shopping list already. If it is, it will remove it by calling `deleteProduct` from the navigation state and also from the component's state by calling `setState`. Otherwise, it will add the product to the shopping list by calling `addProduct` in the navigation state and refresh the local state by calling `setState`.

Finally, we will add an event handler for the delete icon on each of the `<ListItems>`, so the user can remove products from the list of available products:

```
/*** AddProduct.js ***/

...
async _handleRemovePress(product) {
  this.setState({
    allProducts: this.state.allProducts.filter(p => p.id !== product.id)
  });
  await AsyncStorage.setItem(
    '@allProducts',
    JSON.stringify(
      this.state.allProducts.filter(p => p.id !== product.id)
    )
  );
}
...
```

We need to remove the product from the component's local state, but also from the `AsyncStorage` so it doesn't show during later runs of our app.

Putting it all together

We have all the pieces to build our `AddProduct` screen, so let's take a look at the general structure of this component:

```
import React from 'react';
import prompt from 'react-native-prompt-android';
import { AsyncStorage } from 'react-native';
import {
  ...
} from 'native-base';
```

```
export default class AddProduct extends React.Component {
  static navigationOptions = {
    title: 'Add a product'
  };

  constructor(props) {
    ...
  }

  async componentWillMount() {
    ...
  }

  async addNewProduct(name) {
    ...
  }

  /*** User Actions Handlers ***/
  _handleProductPress(product) {
    ...
  }

  _handleAddProductPress() {
    ...
  }

  async _handleRemovePress(product) {
    ...
  }

  /*** Render ***/
  render() {
    ....
  }
}
```

We have a very similar structure to the one we built for `ShoppingList` :
the `navigatorOptions` constructor building the initial state, user action handlers, and a
`render` method. In this case, we added a couple of async methods as a convenient way to
deal with `AsyncStorage`.

Installing and distributing the app

Running our app on a simulator/emulator is a very reliable way to feel how our app will behave in a mobile device. We can simulate touch gestures, poor network connectivity environments, or even memory problems, when working in simulators/emulators. But eventually, we would like to deploy the app to a physical device, so we could perform a more in-depth testing.

There are several options to install or distribute an app built in React Native, the direct cable connection being the easiest one. Facebook keeps an updated guide on how to achieve direct installation on React Native's site (`https://facebook.github.io/react-native/docs/running-on-device.html`), but there are other alternatives when the time comes to distribute the app to other developers, testers, or designated users.

Testflight

Testflight (`https://developer.apple.com/testflight/`) is an awesome tool for distributing the app to beta testers and developers, but it comes with a big drawback--it only works for iOS. It's really simple to set up and use as it is integrated into iTunes Connect, and Apple considers it the official tool for distributing apps within the development team. On top of that, it's absolutely free, and it's usage limits are quite large:

- Up to 25 testers in your team
- Up to 30 devices per tester in your team
- Up to 2,000 external testers outside your team (with grouping capabilities)

In short, Testflight is the platform to choose when you target your apps only to iOS devices.

Since, in this book, we want to focus on cross-platform development, we will introduce other alternatives to distribute our apps to iOS and Android devices from the same platform.

Diawi

Diawi (`http://diawi.com`) is a website where developers can upload their `.ipa` and `.apk` files (the compiled app) and share the links with anybody, so the app can be downloaded and installed on any iOS or Android device connected to the internet. The process is simple:

1. Build the `.ipa` (iOS) / `.apk` (Android) in XCode/Android studio.
2. Drag and drop the generated `.ipa`/`.apk` file into Diawi's site.
3. Share the link created by Diawi with the list of testers by email or any other method.

Links are private and can be password protected for those apps with the higher need of security. The main downside is the management of the testing devices, as once the links are distributed, Diawi loses control over them, so the developer cannot know which versions were downloaded and tested. If managing the list of testers manually is an option, Diawi is a good alternative to Testflight.

Installr

If we are in need of managing what versions were distributed to which testers and whether they have already started testing the app or not, we should give Installr (`https://www.installrapp.com`) a try, since functionality-wise it is quite similar to Diawi, but it also includes a dashboard to control who are the users, which apps were sent to them individually, and the status of the app in the testing device (not installed, installed, or opened). This dashboard is quite powerful and definitely a big plus when one of our requirements is to have good visibility over our testers, devices, and builds.

The downside of Installr is its free plan only covers three testing devices per build, although they offer a cheap one-time pay scheme in case we really want to have that number increased. It's a very reasonable option when we are in need of visibility and cross-platform distribution.

Summary

During the course of this chapter, we learned how to start up a React Native project, building an app which includes basic navigation and handling several user interactions. We saw how to handle persistent data and basic states using the navigation module, so we could transition through the screens in our project.

All these patterns can be used to build lots of simple apps, but in the next chapter, we will dive deeper into more complex navigation patterns and how to communicate and process external data fetched from the internet, which will enable us to structure and prepare our app for growing. On top of that, we will use MobX, a JavaScript library, for state management, which will make our domain data available to all the screens inside our app in a very simple and effective way.

2
RSS Reader

In this chapter, we will create an app which will be able to fetch, process, and show the user several RSS feeds. RSS is a web feed, which allows users to access updates to online content in a standardized and computer-readable format. They are normally used in news websites, news aggregators, forums, and blogs to represent updated content and it fits very well to the mobile world, as we can have all the content from different blogs or newspapers just by entering the feed's URL in one app.

An RSS feed reader will serve as an example on how to fetch external data, store it, and display it to the user, but at the same time, will add a bit of complexity to our state tree; we will need to store and manage lists of feeds, entries, and posts. On top of that, we will introduce MobX as a library to manage all those state models and update our views, based on the user's actions. Therefore, we will introduce the concept of actions and stores, which is widely used in some of the most popular state management libraries, such as Redux or MobX.

As we did in the previous chapter, and because the UI patterns we will need for this app are very similar on both platforms, we will aim at sharing 100% of the code for iOS and Android.

Overview

To better understand our RSS reader, let's take a look at how the app will look like once we finish it.

iOS:

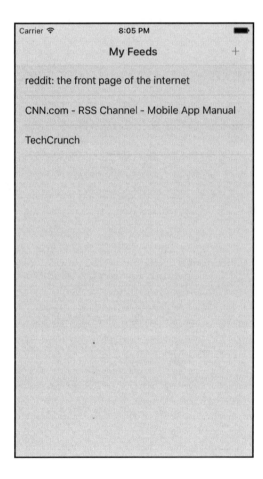

Android:

The home screen will display a list of the feeds already added by the user. It will also show a button (+) in the navigation header to add a new feed to the list. When that button is pressed, the app will navigate to the **Add feed** screen.

iOS:

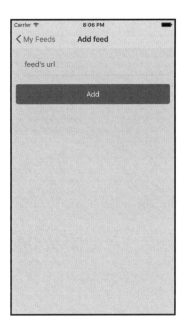

Android:

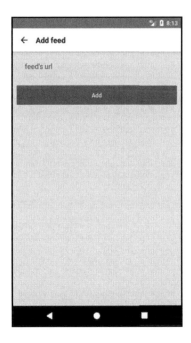

Once a new feed has been added, it will show on the home screen and the user will be able to open it by simply tapping on it.

iOS:

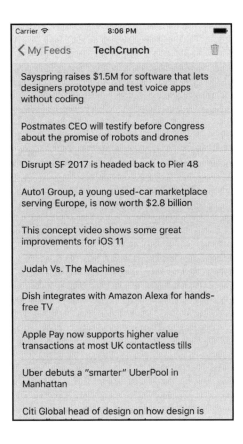

Android:

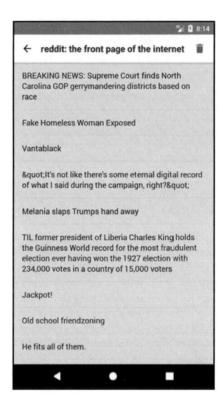

At this stage, the app will retrieve the list of the updated entries for the selected feed and display it on a list. In the navigation header, a Trash icon will allow the user to remove the feed from the app. If the user is interested in any entries, she can click on it to display the full content for that entry.

iOS:

Android:

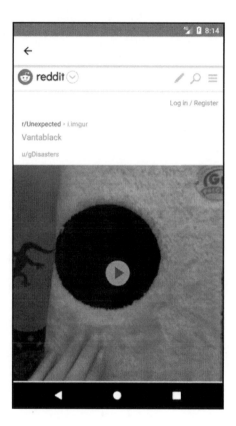

This last screen is basically a WebView, a lightweight browser opened by default in the URL, which is containing the content for the selected entry. The user will be able to navigate to subsections and fully interact with the open website in this screen having also the possibility to go back to the feed details by tapping on the Back arrow in the navigation header.

We will be covering the following topics in this chapter:

- State management with MobX
- Fetch external data from a URL
- WebView
- Basic linking modules with native resources
- Adding icons
- ActivityIndicator

Setting up the folder structure

As we did in the first chapter, we need to initialize a new React Native project through React Native's CLI. This time, we will name our project RSSReader:

```
react-native init --version="0.49.3" RSSReader
```

For this app, we will need a total of four screens:

- FeedList: This is a list containing the titles for the feeds which were added to the app sorted by the time they were added.
- AddFeed: This is a simple form to allow the user to add a feed by sending its URL. We will here retrieve the feed details to finally add and save them in our app for later usage.
- FeedDetail: This is a list containing the latest entries (retrieved before mounting the screen) belonging to the selected feed.
- EntryDetail: This is a WebView showing the contents of the selected entry.

Besides the screens, we will include an actions.js file containing all the user actions modifying the app's state. Although we will review how the state is managed in a later section, in detail, it's also important to note that besides this actions.js file, we need a store.js file to contain the state structure and methods to modify it.

Finally, and as it is normal in most of the React Native projects, we will need an index.js file (already created by React Native's CLI) and a main.js file to serve as an entry point for our app's components tree.

All these files will be organized inside `src/` and `src/screens/` folders, as follows:

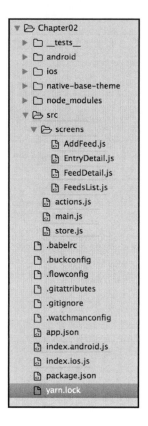

Adding dependencies

For this project, we will use several npm modules to save development time and put the focus on the functional aspects of the RSS reader itself, rather than dealing with custom state management frameworks, custom UI, or data processing. For these matters, we will use the following `package.json` file:

```json
{
    "name":"rssReader",
    "version":"0.0.1",
    "private":true,
    "scripts":{
        "start":"node node_modules/react-native/local-cli/cli.js start",
        "test":"jest"
```

```
    },
    "dependencies":{
        "mobx":"^3.1.9",
        "mobx-react":"^4.1.8",
        "native-base":"^2.1.3",
        "react":"16.0.0-beta.5",
        "react-native": "0.49.3",
        "react-native-vector-icons":"^4.1.1",
        "react-navigation":"^1.0.0-beta.9",
        "simple-xml2json":"^1.2.3"
    },
    "devDependencies":{
        "babel-jest":"20.0.0",
        "babel-plugin-transform-decorators-legacy":"^1.3.4",
        "babel-preset-react-native":"1.9.1",
        "babel-preset-react-native-stage-0":"^1.0.1",
        "jest":"20.0.0",
        "react-test-renderer":"16.0.0-alpha.6"
    },
    "jest":{
        "preset":"react-native"
    }
}
```

As can be seen in this file, we will be using the following npm modules together with the standard React Native's modules:

- mobx: This is the state management library we will be using
- mobx-react: This is the official React bindings for MobX
- native-base: As we did in the previous chapter, we will use NativeBase's UI library
- react-native-vector-icons: NativeBase requires this module to display graphic icons
- react-navigation: We will use the React Native's community navigation library again
- simple-xml2json: A lightweight library to convert XML (the standard format for RSS feeds) into JSON to easily manage the RSS data within our code

Having this package.json file, we can run the following command (in the root folder of our project) to finish the installation:

```
npm install
```

Once npm finishes installing all dependencies, we can start our app in the iOS simulator:

```
react-native run-ios
```

Or in the Android emulator:

```
react-native run-android
```

Using vector icons

For this app, we will use two icons: a plus sign to add feeds and a trash bin to remove them. React Native doesn't include a list of icons to be used by default, so we will need to add one. In our case, since we are using `native-base` as our UI library, it's very convenient to use `react-native-vector-icons`, as it is supported natively from `native-base`, but it requires one extra configuration step:

```
react-native link
```

Some libraries use extra native capabilities which are not present in React Native. In the case of `react-native-vector-icons`, we need to include a number of vector icons stored in the library accessible natively. For these kinds of tasks, React Native includes `react-native link`, a script to automatically link the provided library to prepare all the native code and resources, which are needed for this library to be accessible within our app. Lots of libraries will require this extra step, but thanks to React Native's CLI, it is a very simple step, which in the past required moving files around projects and messing with configuration options.

Managing our state with MobX

MobX is a library which makes state management simple and scalable by transparently applying functional reactive programming. The philosophy behind MobX is very simple: *anything that can be derived from the application state, should be derived automatically.* This philosophy applies to UI, data serialisation and server communication.

Lots of documentation and examples of using MobX can be found on its website `https://mobx.js.org/`, although we will make a small introduction in this section to fully understand our app's code in this chapter.

The store

MobX uses the concept of "observable" properties. We should declare an object containing our general application's state, which will hold and declare those observable properties. When we modify one of these properties, all the subscribed observers will be updated by MobX automatically. This is the basic principle behind MobX, so let's take a look at a sample code:

```
/*** src/store.js ***/

import {observable} from 'mobx';

class Store {
  @observable feeds;

  ...

  constructor() {
    this.feeds = [];
  }

  addFeed(url, feed) {
    this.feeds.push({
      url,
      entry: feed.entry,
      title: feed.title,
      updated: feed.updated
    });
    this._persistFeeds();
  }

  ...

}

const store = new Store()
export default store
```

We have an attribute, feeds, marked as @observable, meaning that any component can subscribe to it and be notified every time the value is changed. This attribute is initialized as an empty array in the class constructor.

Finally, we also created the `addFeed` method, which will push a new feed into the `feeds` attribute and therefore will trigger automatic updates on all the observers. To better understand MobX observers, let's take a look at a sample component observing the feeds list:

```
import React from 'react';
import { Container, Content, List, ListItem, Text } from 'native-base';
import { observer } from 'mobx-react/native';

@observer
export default class FeedsList extends React.Component {

  render() {
   const { feeds } = this.props.screenProps.store;
   return (
     <Container>
       <Content>
         <List>
           {feeds &&
             feeds.map((f, i) => (
               <ListItem key={i}>
                 <Text>{f.title}</Text>
               </ListItem>
             ))}
         </List>
       </Content>
     </Container>
   );
  }
}
```

The first thing we notice is the need to mark our component with the `@observer` decorator to ensure it is updated when any of the `@observable` properties change in our store.

 By default, React Native's Babel configuration doesn't support the `@<decorator>` syntax. In order for it to work, we will need to modify our `.babelrc` file (found in the root of our project) and add `transform-decorator-legacy` as a plugin.

Another thing to note is the need for the store to be received in the component as a property. In this case, since we are using `react-navigation`, we will pass it inside `screenProps`, which is the standard way in `react-navigation` for sharing properties between `<Navigator>` and its child screens.

MobX has many more features, but we will leave those for more complex apps as one of the goals for this chapter is to show how simple state management can be when we are building small apps.

Setting up the store

After understanding how MobX works, we are ready to create our store:

```
/*** src/store.js ** */

import { observable } from 'mobx';
import { AsyncStorage } from 'react-native';

class Store {
  @observable feeds;
  @observable selectedFeed;
  @observable selectedEntry;

  constructor() {
    AsyncStorage.getItem('@feeds').then(sFeeds => {
      this.feeds = JSON.parse(sFeeds) || [];
    });
  }

  _persistFeeds() {
    AsyncStorage.setItem('@feeds', JSON.stringify(this.feeds));
  }

  addFeed(url, feed) {
    this.feeds.push({
      url,
      entry: feed.entry,
      title: feed.title,
      updated: feed.updated,
    });
    this._persistFeeds();
  }

  removeFeed(url) {
    this.feeds = this.feeds.filter(f => f.url !== url);
    this._persistFeeds();
  }

  selectFeed(feed) {
    this.selectedFeed = feed;
  }
```

```
    selectEntry(entry) {
      this.selectedEntry = entry;
    }
  }

  const store = new Store();
  export default store;
```

We have already seen the basic structure of this file in the MobX section of this chapter. Now, we will add some methods to modify the list of feeds and to select a specific feed/entry when the user taps on them in our app's listings for feeds/entries.

We are also making use of `AsyncStorage` to persist the list of feeds every time it is modified by either `addFeed` or `removeFeed`.

Defining actions

There will be two types of actions in our app: those affecting a specific component's state and those affecting the general app state. We want to store the latter somewhere out of the component's code, so we can reuse and easily maintain them. An extended practice in MobX (and also Redux or Flux) apps is to create a file named `actions.js`, where we will store all the actions modifying business logic for our app.

In the case of our RSS reader, the business logic revolves around feeds and entries, so we will capture all the logic dealing with these models in this file:

```
/*** actions.js ** */

import store from './store';
import xml2json from 'simple-xml2json';

export async function fetchFeed(url) {
  const response = await fetch(url);
  const xml = await response.text();
  const json = xml2json.parser(xml);
  return {
    entry:
      (json.feed && json.feed.entry) || (json.rss &&
      json.rss.channel.item),
    title:
      (json.feed && json.feed.title) || (json.rss &&
      json.rss.channel.title),
    updated: (json.feed && json.feed.updated) || null,
  };
}
```

```
export function selectFeed(feed) {
  store.selectFeed(feed);
}

export function selectEntry(entry) {
  store.selectEntry(entry);
}

export function addFeed(url, feed) {
  store.addFeed(url, feed);
}

export function removeFeed(url) {
  store.removeFeed(url);
}
```

Since actions modify the general app state, they will need to access the store. Let's take a look at each action separately:

- fetchFeed: When a user wants to add a feed to the RSS reader, he will need to pass the URL, so the app can download the details for that feed (feed title, list of latest entries, and when it was updated for the last time). This action is responsible for retrieving this data (formatted as an XML document) from the supplied URL and transforming that data into a JSON object with a standard format for the app. Fetching the data from the supplied URL will be performed by fetch, a built-in library in React Native, which is used to make HTTP requests to any URL. Since fetch supports promises, we will use async/await to handle the asynchronous behavior and simplify our code. Once the XML document containing the feed's data is retrieved, we will convert that data into a JSON object using simple-xml2json, a very lightweight library for this kind of needs. Finally, the action returns a JSON object containing only the data we will really need in our app (title, entries, and last update time).
- selectFeed: Once the user has added one or more feeds to the reader, she should be able to select one of them to get the list of the latest entries for that feed. This action just saves the details for a specific feed in the store, so it can be used by any screen interested in displaying data related to that feed (that is, the FeedDetail screen).
- selectEntry: Similar to selectFeed, a user should be able to select one of the entries in a feed to get the details for that specific entry. In this case, the screen displaying that data will be EntryDetail as we will see in a later section.

- `addFeed`: This action requires two parameters: the URL for a feed and the feed's detail. These parameters will be used to store the feed in the list of saved feeds so that it will be available globally in our app. In the case of this app, we decided to use the URL as the key which stores the details for the feed, as it is a unique property of any RSS feed.
- `removeFeed`: A user can also decide that they don't want a specific feed in the RSS reader anymore and therefore we need an action to remove the feed from the list of feeds. This action only requires the URL for the feed to be passed as a parameter, since we stored the feed using the URL as an ID to uniquely identify the feed.

Networking in React Native

Most mobile apps need to fetch and update data from an external URL. There are several npm modules, which can be used in React Native to communicate and download remote resources such as Axios or SuperAgent. If you are familiar with a specific HTTP library, you can use it in your React Native projects (as long as is not dependent on any browser specific APIs), although a safe and proficient option is to use `Fetch`, the built-in networking library in React Native.

`Fetch` is very similar to `XMLHttpRequest`, so it will feel familiar to any web developers who had to perform AJAX requests from the browser. On top of that, `Fetch` supports promises and the ES2017 async/await syntax.

The full documentation for the `Fetch` API can be found on Mozilla Developer Networks website `https://developer.mozilla.org/en-US/docs/Web/API/Fetch_API`.

 By default, iOS will block any request that's not encrypted using SSL. If you need to fetch from a cleartext URL (one that begins with `http` instead of `https`), you will first need to add an **App Transport Security** (**ATS**) exception. If you know ahead of time what domains you will need access to, it is more secure to add exceptions just for those domains; if the domains are not known until runtime, you can disable ATS completely. Note, however, that from January 2017, Apple's App Store review will require reasonable justification for disabling ATS. See Apple's documentation for more information.

Creating our app's entry point

All React Native apps have one entry file: `index.js`, we will delegate the root of the component's tree to our `src/main.js` file:

```
/*** index.js ***/

import { AppRegistry } from 'react-native';
import App from './src/main';
AppRegistry.registerComponent('rssReader', () => App);
```

We will also register our app with the operating system.

Now, let's take a look at the `src/main.js` file to understand how we will set up navigation and start up our component's tree:

```
/** * src/main.js ***/

import React from 'react';
import { StackNavigator } from 'react-navigation';

import FeedsList from './screens/FeedsList.js';
import FeedDetail from './screens/FeedDetail.js';
import EntryDetail from './screens/EntryDetail.js';
import AddFeed from './screens/AddFeed.js';

import store from './store';

const Navigator = StackNavigator({
  FeedsList: { screen: FeedsList },
  FeedDetail: { screen: FeedDetail },
  EntryDetail: { screen: EntryDetail },
  AddFeed: { screen: AddFeed },
});

export default class App extends React.Component {
  constructor() {
    super();
  }

  render() {
    return <Navigator screenProps={{ store }} />;
  }
}
```

We will use `react-navigation` as our navigator library and `StackNavigator` as our navigation pattern. Add each of our screens to the `StackNavigator` function to generate our `<Navigator>`. All this is very similar to the navigation pattern we used in Chapter 1, *Shopping List*, but we incorporated an improvement to it: we are passing `store` in the `screenProps` property for our `<Navigator>`, instead of directly passing the attributes and methods to modify our app's state. This simplifies and cleans up the code base and as we will see in later sections, it will free us from notifying the navigation every time our state changes. All these improvements come for free thanks to MobX.

Building the FeedsList screen

The list of feeds will be used as the home screen for this app, so let's focus on building the list of the feeds' titles:

```
/** * src/screens/FeedsList.js ***/

import React from 'react';
import { Container, Content, List, ListItem, Text } from 'native-base';

export default class FeedsList extends React.Component {
  render() {
    const { feeds } = this.props.screenProps.store;
    return (
      <Container>
        <Content>
          <List>
            {feeds &&
              feeds.map((f, i) => (
              <ListItem key={i}>
              <Text>{f.title}</Text>
              </ListItem>
              ))}
          </List>
        </Content>
      </Container>
    );
  }
}
```

This component expects to receive the list of feeds from `this.props.screenProps.store` and then iterates over that list building a NativeBase `<List>`, showing the titles for each of the feeds on the store.

Let's introduce some MobX magic now. As we want our component to be re-rendered when the list of feeds changes (when a feed is added or removed), we have to mark our component with the `@observer` decorator. MobX will automatically force the component re-rendering on any update. Let's see now how to add the decorator to our component:

```
...

@observer
export default class FeedsList extends React.Component {

...
```

That's it. Now, our component will be notified when the store is changed and a re-render will be triggered.

Adding event handlers

Let's add an event handler to be triggered when the user taps on one of the feed's titles so the list of entries for that feed is displayed on a new screen (`FeedDetail`):

```
/** * src/screens/FeedsList.js ***/

...

@observer
export default class FeedsList extends React.Component {
  _handleFeedPress(feed) {
    selectFeed(feed);
    this.props.navigation.navigate('FeedDetail', { feedUrl: feed.url });
  }

  render() {
    const { feeds } = this.props.screenProps.store;
    return (
      <Container>
        <Content>
          <List>
            {feeds &&
              feeds.map((f, i) => (
              <ListItem key={i} onPress=
              {this._handleFeedPress.bind(this, f)}>
              <Text>{f.title}</Text>
              </ListItem>
            ))
            }
          </List>
```

```
          </Content>
        </Container>
      );
    }
  }
```

. . .

For this, we added a method to our component named _handleFeedPress, which will receive the feed detail as a parameter. When this method is called, it will run the action selectFeed and will trigger a navigation event passing the feed's URL as a property, so the next screen (FeedDetail) can include a button to delete the feed based on that URL.

Finally, we will add navigationOptions, including the title for the navigation header and the button to add a feed:

```
/** * src/screens/FeedsList.js ***/

...

@observer
export default class FeedsList extends React.Component {
  static navigationOptions = props => ({
    title: 'My Feeds',
    headerRight: (
      <Button transparent onPress={() =>
      props.navigation.navigate('AddFeed')}>
        <Icon name="add" />
      </Button>
    ),
  });

...

}
```

Pressing the AddFeed button will navigate to the AddFeed screen. This button will be displayed to the right of the navigation header by passing it as a property named headerRight in the navigationOptions.

Let's see how this component looks all together:

```
/*** src/screens/FeedsList.js ** */

import React from 'react';
import {
  Container,
  Content,
  List,
  ListItem,
  Text,
  Icon,
  Button,
} from 'native-base';
import { observer } from 'mobx-react/native';
import { selectFeed, removeFeed } from '../actions';

@observer
export default class FeedsList extends React.Component {
  static navigationOptions = props => ({
    title: 'My Feeds',
    headerRight: (
      <Button transparent onPress={() =>
       props.navigation.navigate('AddFeed')}>
        <Icon name="add" />
      </Button>
    ),
  });

  _handleFeedPress(feed) {
    selectFeed(feed);
    this.props.navigation.navigate('FeedDetail', { feedUrl: feed.url });
  }

  render() {
    const { feeds } = this.props.screenProps.store;
    return (
      <Container>
        <Content>
          <List>
            {feeds &&
              feeds.map((f, i) => (
              <ListItem key={i} onPress=
              {this._handleFeedPress.bind(this, f)}>
              <Text>{f.title}</Text>
              </ListItem>
            ))
          </List>
```

```
        </Content>
      </Container>
    );
  }
}
```

Now that we have our list of feeds fully functional, let's allow the users to add some feeds through the AddFeed screen.

Building the AddFeed screen

This screen consists of a basic form, including one <Input> for the URL from the feed and a <Button> to retrieve the feed information from the provided URL to later store the feed's details in our store.

We will need to import two actions (addFeed and fetchFeed), which will be called once the Add button is pressed:

```
/*** src/screens/AddFeed.js ** */

import React from 'react';
import {
  Container,
  Content,
  Form,
  Item,
  Input,
  Button,
  Text,
} from 'native-base';
import { addFeed, fetchFeed } from '../actions';
import { Alert, ActivityIndicator } from 'react-native';

export default class AddFeed extends React.Component {
  static navigationOptions = {
    title: 'Add feed',
  };

  constructor(props) {
    super(props);
    this.state = {
      url: '',
      loading: false,
    };
  }
```

```
_handleAddPress() {
  if (this.state.url.length > 0) {
    this.setState({ loading: true });
    fetchFeed(this.state.url)
      .then(feed => {
        addFeed(this.state.url, feed);
        this.setState({ loading: false });
        this.props.navigation.goBack();
      })
      .catch(() => {
        Alert.alert("Couldn't find any rss feed on that url");
        this.setState({ loading: false });
      });
  }
}

render() {
  return (
    <Container style={{ padding: 10 }}>
      <Content>
        <Form>
          <Item>
            <Input
              autoCapitalize="none"
              autoCorrect={false}
              placeholder="feed's url"
              onChangeText={url => this.setState({ url })}
            />
          </Item>
          <Button
            block
            style={{ marginTop: 20 }}
            onPress={this._handleAddPress.bind(this)}
          >
            {this.state.loading && (
              <ActivityIndicator color="white" style={{ margin: 10 }}
              />
            )}
            <Text>Add</Text>
          </Button>
        </Form>
      </Content>
    </Container>
  );
}
}
```

Most of the functionality in this component is in _handleAddPress as it is the handler, which will be triggered once the Add button is pushed. This handler is responsible for four tasks:

- Checking there is a URL present to retrieve data from
- Retrieving the feed data from the provided URL (through the fetchFeed action)
- Saving that data into the app's state (through the addFeed action)
- Alerting the user if something went wrong when fetching or saving the data.

One important thing to note is how the fetchFeed action is used. Since it was declared with the async syntax, we can use it as a promise and attach it to the result of its listeners for then and catch.

ActivityIndicator

It is a good practice to display a spinner every time the app needs to wait for a response to an HTTP request. Both iOS and Android have standard activity indicators to display this behavior and both are available through the <ActivityIndicator> component in React Native's module.

The easiest way to display this indicator is by keeping a loading flag in the component state. Since this flag is only used by our component to display this <ActivityIndicator>, it makes sense to have it inside the component's state instead of moving it to the general app's state. Then, it can be used inside the render function:

```
{ this.state.loading && <ActivityIndicator color='white' style={{margin:
10}}/>}
```

This syntax is very common in React apps for displaying or hiding components based on flags or simple conditions. It takes advantage of the way JavaScript evaluates the && operations: check truthiness of the first operand, if truthy, returns the second operator; otherwise, it returns the first operator. This syntax saves lines of code on a very common kind of instructions and therefore it will be widely used throughout this book.

Building the FeedDetail screen

Let's recap what happened when the user tapped on one feed on the FeedsList screen:

```
_handleFeedPress(feed) {
  selectFeed(feed);
  this.props.navigation.navigate('FeedDetail', { feedUrl: feed.url });
}
```

The navigate method was called on the navigation property to open the FeedDetail screen. As a parameter, the _handleFeedPress function passed feedUrl, so it can retrieve the feed data and display it to the user. This is a necessary step since the data we have in our store for the selected feed can be obsolete. So, it's better to re-fetch that data before showing it to the user so we are sure it's 100% updated. We could also do a more complex check instead of retrieving the whole feed every time the user selects a feed, but we will stay with the given approach in order to keep simplicity in this app.

Let's start by retrieving the updated list of entries in the componentWillMount method:

```
/*** src/screens/FeedDetail.js ***/

import React from 'react';
import { observer } from 'mobx-react/native';
import { fetchFeed} from '../actions';

@observer
export default class FeedDetail extends React.Component {
  ...

  constructor (props) {
   super(props);
   this.state = {
     loading: false,
     entry: null
   }
  }

  componentWillMount() {
   this.setState({ loading: true });
   fetchFeed(this.props.screenProps.store.selectedFeed.url)
     .then((feed) => {
     this.setState({ loading: false });
     this.setState({ entry: feed.entry});
    });
  }
```

```
    . . .

}
```

We will mark our component as @observer so that it get's updated every time the selected feed changes. Then, we need a state with two properties:

- loading: This is a flag to signal to the user that we are fetching the updated feed's data
- entry: This is the list of entries to be displayed to the user

Then, before the component is mounted, we want to start the retrieval of the updated entries. For this matter, we can reuse the fetchFeed action we used in the AddFeed screen. When the feed data is received, the loading flag in the component's state is set to false, which will hide <ActivityIndicator> and the entries list for the feed will be set in the component's state. Now that we have a list of entries, let's take a look at how we will display it to the user:

```
/** * src/screens/FeedDetail.js ** */

import React from 'react';
import {
  Container,
  Content,
  List,
  ListItem,
  Text,
  Button,
  Icon,
  Spinner,
} from 'native-base';
import { observer } from 'mobx-react/native';
import { fetchFeed } from '../actions';
import { ActivityIndicator } from 'react-native';

@observer
export default class FeedDetail extends React.Component {

  ...

  render() {
    const { entry } = this.state;

    return (
      <Container>
        <Content>
```

```
            {this.state.loading && <ActivityIndicator style=
            {{ margin: 20 }} />}
            <List>
              {entry &&
                entry.map((e, i) => (
                  <ListItem key={i}>
                    <Text>{e.title}</Text>
                  </ListItem>
              ))}
            </List>
          </Content>
        </Container>
      );
    }
  }
```

The `&&` syntax is used again to display `<ActivityIndicator>` until the data is retrieved. Once the data is available and properly stored in, the `entry` property inside our component's state, we will render the list items containing the entries titles for the selected field.

Now, we will add an event handler which will be triggered when a user taps on one of the entries' titles:

```
/** * src/screens/FeedDetail.js ** */

import React from 'react';
import {
  Container,
  Content,
  List,
  ListItem,
  Text,
  Button,
  Icon,
  Spinner,
} from 'native-base';
import { observer } from 'mobx-react/native';
import { selectEntry, fetchFeed } from '../actions';
import { ActivityIndicator } from 'react-native';

@observer
export default class FeedDetail extends React.Component {

  ...

  _handleEntryPress(entry) {
```

```
      selectEntry(entry);
      this.props.navigation.navigate('EntryDetail');
   }

   render() {
     const { entry } = this.state;

     return (
       <Container>
         <Content>
           {this.state.loading && <ActivityIndicator style=
           {{ margin: 20 }} />}
           <List>
             {entry &&
               entry.map((e, i) => (
                 <ListItem
                   key={i}
                   onPress={this._handleEntryPress.bind(this, e)}
                 >
                   <Text>{e.title}</Text>
                 </ListItem>
               ))}
           </List>
         </Content>
       </Container>
     );
   }
}
```

This handler is named _handleEntryPress and is responsible for two tasks:

- Marking the tapped entry as selected
- Navigating to EntryDetail

To finalize the component, let's add the navigation header through the navigationOptions method:

```
/** * src/screens/FeedDetail.js ** */

...

@observer
export default class FeedDetail extends React.Component {
  static navigationOptions = props => ({
    title: props.screenProps.store.selectedFeed.title,
    headerRight: (
      <Button
```

```
            transparent
            onPress={() => {
              removeFeed(props.navigation.state.params.feedUrl);
              props.navigation.goBack();
            }}
          >
            <Icon name="trash" />
          </Button>
        ),
      });

      ...
    }
```

Besides adding the title for this screen (the feed's title), we want to add an icon to the navigation for the user to be able to remove the feed from the stored list of feeds in the app. We will use the trash icon of native-base for this purpose. When it's pressed, the removeFeed action will be called passing the URL for the current feed URL, so it can be deleted from the store, then it will force the navigation to go back to the FeedList screen.

Let's take a look at the finished component:

```
/*** src/screens/FeedDetail.js ** */

import React from 'react';
import {
  Container,
  Content,
  List,
  ListItem,
  Text,
  Button,
  Icon,
  Spinner,
} from 'native-base';
import { observer } from 'mobx-react/native';
import { selectEntry, fetchFeed, removeFeed } from '../actions';
import { ActivityIndicator } from 'react-native';

@observer
export default class FeedDetail extends React.Component {
  static navigationOptions = props => ({
    title: props.screenProps.store.selectedFeed.title,
    headerRight: (
      <Button
        transparent
        onPress={() => {
```

```
          removeFeed(props.navigation.state.params.feedUrl);
          props.navigation.goBack();
        }}
      >
        <Icon name="trash" />
      </Button>
    ),
  });

  constructor(props) {
    super(props);
    this.state = {
      loading: false,
      entry: null,
    };
  }

  componentWillMount() {
    this.setState({ loading: true });
    fetchFeed(this.props.screenProps.store.selectedFeed.url).
    then(feed => {
      this.setState({ loading: false });
      this.setState({ entry: feed.entry });
    });
  }

  _handleEntryPress(entry) {
    selectEntry(entry);
    this.props.navigation.navigate('EntryDetail');
  }

  render() {
    const { entry } = this.state;

    return (
      <Container>
        <Content>
          {this.state.loading && <ActivityIndicator style=
          {{ margin: 20 }} />}
          <List>
            {entry &&
              entry.map((e, i) => (
              <ListItem key={i} onPress=
              {this._handleEntryPress.bind(this, e)}>
              <Text>{e.title}</Text>
            </ListItem>
            ))
            </List>
```

```
        </Content>
      </Container>
    );
  }
}
```

Now, let's move on to the last screen: `EntryDetail`.

Building the EntryDetail screen

The `EntryDetail` screen is just WebView: a component-abled rendering web content in a native view. You can think of a WebView as a lightweight web browser displaying the contents of a website for a provided URL:

```
import React from 'react';
import { Container, Content } from 'native-base';
import { WebView } from 'react-native';

export default class EntryDetail extends React.Component {
  render() {
    const entry = this.props.screenProps.store.selectedEntry;
    return <WebView source={{ uri: entry.link.href || entry.link }} />;
  }
}
```

The `render` method in this component is merely returning a new `WebView` component loading the URL from the selected entry inside the store. As we did with the feed's data in the previous sections, we need to retrieve the `selectedEntry` data from `this.props.screenProps.store`. The URL can be stored in two different ways depending on the RSS version of the feed: in the link property or one level deeper in `link.href`.

Summary

A state management library becomes necessary in every app when its complexity starts to grow. As a rule of thumb, it's a good idea to add a state management library when the app is comprised of more than four screens and they share information between them. For this app, we used MobX, which is simple but powerful enough to handle all the feeds and entries' data. In this chapter, you learned the basics of MobX and how to use it in conjunction of `react-navigation`. It's important to understand the concept of actions and stores, as we will use them in future apps not only built around MobX but also on Redux.

You also learned how to fetch data from a remote URL. This is a very common action in most of the mobile apps, although we only covered the basic usage of it. In the following chapters, we will dive deeper into the `Fetch` API. Moreover, we saw how to process and format the fetched data to formalize it within our app.

Finally, we reviewed what a WebView is and how we can insert web content into our native app. This can be done using local HTML strings or remotely through the URL, so it's a very powerful trick used by mobile developers to reuse or access web-only content.

3
Car Booking App

In the previous chapters, we set the focus on feature development rather than in building a user interface by delegating the styling of our apps to UI libraries such as `native-base`. In this chapter, we are going to do the opposite and spend more time in building custom UI components and screens.

The app we will build is a car booking app in which the user can select the location in which he/she wants to be picked up and the type of car she wants to book for the ride. Since we want to focus on the user interface, our app will only have two screens and a little state management is needed. Instead, we will dive deeper into aspects such as animations, component's layout, using custom fonts, or displaying external images.

The app will be available for iOS and Android devices, and since all the user interface will be custom made, 100% of the code will be reused between both platforms. We will only use two external libraries:

- `React-native-geocoder`: This will translate coordinates into human-readable locations
- `React-native-maps`: This will easily display the maps and the markers showing the locations for the bookable cars

Due to its nature, most of the car booking apps put their complexity in the backend code to connect drivers with riders effectively. We will skip this complexity and mock all that functionality in the app itself to focus on building beautiful and usable interfaces.

Overview

When building mobile apps, we need to make sure we reduce the interface complexity to the minimum, as it's often punishing to present the user intrusive manuals or tooltips once the app is open. It is a good practice to make our app self-explanatory, so the user can understand the usage just by going through the app screens. That's why using standard components such as drawer menus or standard lists is always a good idea, but is not always possible (as it happens in our current app) due to the kind of data we want to present to the user.

In our case, we put all the functionality in the main screen plus in a modal box. Let's take a look at what the app will look like on iOS devices:

The background on our main screen is the maps component itself where we will show all the available cars as markers in the map. On the maps, we will display three components:

- The pickup location box displaying the selected pickup location
- The location pin, which can be dragged around the maps to select a new location
- The selector for the kind of car the user wants to book. We will display three options: **ECONOMY**, **SPECIAL**, and **SUPERIOR**

Since most of the components are custom built, this screen will look very similar in any Android device:

The main difference between the iOS and the Android version will be the map component. While iOS will use Apple maps by default, Android uses Google Maps. We will leave this setup as each platform has its own map component optimized, but it's good to know that we can switch the iOS version to use Google Maps just by configuring our component.

Once the user has selected a pickup location, we will display a modal box to confirm the booking and contact the nearest driver for pickup:

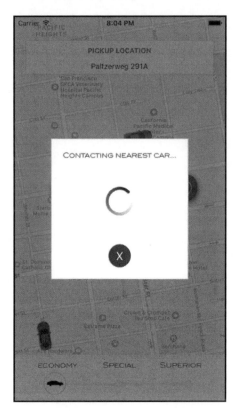

As it happened with the main screen, this screen uses custom components: we even decided to create our own animated activity indicator. Because of this, the Android version will look very similar:

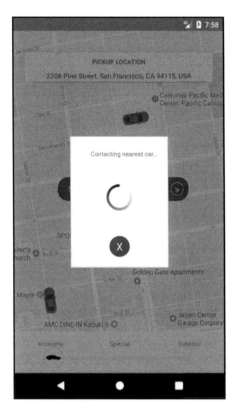

Since our app won't be connected to any external API, it should be seen as a mere display of the visual capabilities of React Native, although it could be easily extended by adding a state management library and a matching API.

We will be covering the following topics in this chapter:

- Using maps in our app
- Style sheets in React Native
- Flexbox in React Native
- Using external images in a React Native app
- Adding custom fonts
- Animations in React Native

- Using modals
- Working with shadows and opacity

Setting up the folder structure

Let's initialize a React Native project using React Native's CLI. The project will be named `carBooking` and will be available for iOS and Android devices:

```
react-native init --version="0.49.3" carBooking
```

In this app, there is only one screen so that the folder structure for the code should be very straightforward. Since we will be using external images and fonts, we will organize these resources in two separate folders: `img` and `fonts`, both under the root folder:

The images and fonts used to build this app can be downloaded freely from some image and font sock websites. The name of the font we will use is *Blair ITC*.

We also stored the following images inside the `img` folder:

- `car.png`: A simple drawing of a car to represent the bookable cars on the map.
- `class.png`: The silhouette of a car to show inside the class selection button.
- `classBar.png`: The bar in which the class selection button will be slid to change the class.
- `loading.png`: Our custom spinner. It will be stored as a static image and animated through the code.

Finally, let's take a look at our `package.json` file:

```json
{
    "name": "carBooking",
    "version": "0.0.1",
    "private": true,
    "scripts": {
        "start": "node node_modules/react-native/local-cli/cli.js start",
        "test": "jest"
    },
    "dependencies": {
        "react": "16.0.0-beta.5",
        "react-native": "0.49.3",
        "react-native-geocoder": "^0.4.8",
        "react-native-maps": "^0.15.2"
    },
    "devDependencies": {
        "babel-jest": "20.0.3",
        "babel-preset-react-native": "1.9.2",
        "jest": "20.0.4",
        "react-test-renderer": "16.0.0-alpha.6"
    },
    "jest": {
        "preset": "react-native"
    },
    "rnpm": {
        "assets": ["./fonts"]
    }
}
```

We only use two npm modules:

- `react-native-geocoder`: This translates coordinates into human-readable locations
- `react-native-maps`: This easily displays the maps and the markers showing the locations for the bookable cars

In order to allow the app to use custom fonts, we need to make sure they are accessible from the native side. For that, we need to add a new key to `package.json` named `rnpm`. This key will store an array of `assets` in which we will define our `fonts` folder. During build time, React Native will copy the fonts to a location from where they will be available natively and therefore usable within our code. This is only required by fonts and some special resources, but not by images.

Files and folders created by React Native's CLI

Let's take the chance of having a simple folder structure in this app to show what other files and folders are created by React Native's CLI when initializing a project through `react-native init <projectName>`.

__tests__/

React Native's CLI includes Jest as a developer dependency and, to get testing started, it includes a folder named `__tests__`, in which all tests can be stored. By default, React Native's CLI adds one test file: `index.js` , representing the initial set of tests. Developers can add later tests for any components in the app. React Native also adds a `test` script in our `package.json`, so we can run `npm run test` from the very first moment.

Jest is ready to be used with every project initialized through the CLI and it's definitely the easiest option when it comes to testing React components, although it is also possible to use other libraries such as Jasmine or Mocha.

android/ and ios/

These two folders hold the built app for both platforms natively. This means that we can find our `.xcodeproj` and `.java` files in here. Every time we need to make changes to the native code of our app, we will need to modify some files in these two directories.

The most common reasons to find and modify files in these folders are:

- Modify permissions (push notifications, access to location services, access to compass, and many more) by changing `Info.plist` (iOS) or `AndroidManifest.xml` (Android)
- Change the build settings for any platform
- Add API keys for native libraries
- Add or modify native libraries to be used from our React Native code

node_modules/

This folder should be familiar to most of the JavaScript developers who worked with npm as it is where npm stores all the modules marked as a dependency in our project. It is not common to have the necessity to modify anything inside this folder, as everything should be handled through npm's CLI and our `package.json` file.

Files in the root folder

React Native's CLI creates a number of files in the root directory of our project; let's take a look at the most important ones:

- `.babelrc`: Babel is the default library in React Native to compile our JavaScript files containing JSX and ES6 (for example, syntax into plain JavaScript capable to be understood by most of the JavaScript engines). Here, we can modify the configuration for this compiler so we can, for example, use the @ syntax for decorators as it was done in the first versions of React.
- `.buckconfig`: Buck is the build system used by Facebook. This file is used to configure the building process when using Buck.
- `.watchmanconfig`: Watchman is a service that watches the files in our project to trigger a rebuild anytime something changes in them. In this file, we can add some configuration options such as directories, which should be ignored.
- `app.json`: This file is used by the `react-native eject` command to configure the native apps. It stores the name that identifies the app in each platform and also the name that will be displayed on the home screen of the device when the app is installed.
- `yarn.lock`: The `package.json` file describes the intended versions desired by the original author, while `yarn.lock` describes the last-known-good configuration for a given application.

react-native link

Some apps depend on libraries with native capabilities which, before React Native CLI, required developers to copy native library files into the native projects. This was a cumbersome and repetitive project until `react-native link` came to the rescue. In this chapter we will use it to copy library files from `react-native-maps` and to link custom fonts from our `/fonts` folder to the compiled app.

By running `react-native link` in our project's root folder we will trigger the linking steps which will result in those native capabilities and resources to be accessible from our React Native code.

Running the app in the simulator

Having the dependencies in the `package.json` file and all the initial files in place, we can run the following command (in the root folder of our project) to finish the installation:

```
npm install
```

Then, all the dependencies should be installed in our project. Once npm finishes installing all dependencies, we can start our app in the iOS simulator:

```
react-native run-ios
```

Or in the Android emulator using the following command:

```
react-native run-android
```

When React Native detects the app is running in a simulator, it enables a developer toolset available through a hidden menu, which can be accessed through the shortcuts *command + D* on iOS or *command + M* on Android (on Windows *Ctrl* should be used instead of *command*). This is how the developer menu looks like in iOS:

And this is how it looks like in the Android simulator:

The developer menu

In the process of building an app in React Native, the developer will have debugging needs. React Native fulfills these needs with the ability to remotely debug our apps in Chrome developer's tools or external applications such as React Native Debugger. Errors, logs, and even React components can be debugged easily as in a normal web environment.

On top of that, React Native provides a way to automatically reload our app each time a change is done saving the developers the task of manually reloading the app (which can be achieved by pressing *command + R* or *Ctrl + R*). There are two options when we set our app for automatic reloading:

- Live reload detects any changes we make in the app's code and resets the app to its initial state after reloading.
- Hot reload also detects changes and reloads the app, but keeps the current state of the app. This is really useful when we are implementing user flows to save the developer to repeat each step in the flow (for example, logging in or registering test users)

Finally, we can start the performance monitor to detect possible performance issues when performing complex operations such as animations or mathematical calculations.

Creating our app's entry point

Let's start our app's code by creating the entry point for our app: `index.js`. We import `src/main.js` in this file to use a common root component for our code base. Moreover, we will register the app with the name `carBooking`:

```
/*** index.js ***/

import { AppRegistry } from 'react-native';
import App from './src/main';
AppRegistry.registerComponent('carBooking', () => App);
```

Let's start building our `src/main.js` by adding a map component:

```
/*** src/main.js ** */

import React from 'react';
import { View, StyleSheet } from 'react-native';
import MapView from 'react-native-maps';
```

```
export default class Main extends React.Component {
  constructor(props) {
    super(props);
    this.initialRegion = {
      latitude: 37.78825,
      longitude: -122.4324,
      latitudeDelta: 0.00922,
      longitudeDelta: 0.00421,
    };
  }

  render() {
    return (
      <View style={{ flex: 1 }}>
        <MapView
          style={styles.fullScreenMap}
          initialRegion={this.initialRegion}
        />
      </View>
    );
  }
}

const styles = StyleSheet.create({
  fullScreenMap: {
    position: 'absolute',
    top: 0,
    bottom: 0,
    left: 0,
    right: 0,
  },
});
```

Instead of using libraries for styling, we will create our own styles using `StyleSheet`, a React Native API, which serves as an abstraction similar to CSS style sheets. With `StyleSheet`, we can create a style sheet from an object (through the `create` method), which can be used in our components by referring to each style by its ID.

This way, we can reuse the style code and make the code more readable as we will be using meaningful names to refer to each style (for example, `<Text style={styles.title}>Title 1</Text>`).

At this point, we will only create a style referred by the key `fullScreenMap` and make it as an absolute position by covering the fullscreen size by adding `top`, `bottom`, `left`, and `right` coordinates to zero. On top of this, we need to add some styling to our container view to ensure it fills the whole screen: `{flex: 1}`. Setting `flex` to 1, we want our view to fill all the space its parent occupies. Since this is the main view, `{flex: 1}` will take over the whole screen.

For our map component, we will use `react-native-maps`, an open module created by Airbnb using native maps capabilities for Google and Apple maps. `react-native-maps` is a very flexible module, really well maintained, and fully featured so that it has become the *de facto* maps module for React Native. As we will see later in this chapter, `react-native-maps` requires the developer to run `react-native link` in order for it to work.

Apart from the style, the `<MapView/>` component will take `initialRegion` as a property to centre the map in a specific set of coordinates, which should be the current location of the user. For consistency reasons, we will locate the center of the map in San Francisco where we will also place some bookable cars:

```
/** * src/main.js ** */

import React from 'react';
import { View, Animated, Image, StyleSheet } from 'react-native';
import MapView from 'react-native-maps';

export default class Main extends React.Component {
  constructor(props) {
    super(props);
    this.state = {
      carLocations: [
        {
          rotation: 78,
          latitude: 37.78725,
          longitude: -122.4318,
        },
        {
          rotation: -10,
          latitude: 37.79015,
          longitude: -122.4318,
        },
        {
          rotation: 262,
          latitude: 37.78525,
          longitude: -122.4348,
        },
      ],
```

```
    };
    this.initialRegion = {
      latitude: 37.78825,
      longitude: -122.4324,
      latitudeDelta: 0.00922,
      longitudeDelta: 0.00421,
    };
  }

  render() {
    return (
      <View style={{ flex: 1 }}>
        <MapView
          style={styles.fullScreenMap}
          initialRegion={this.initialRegion}
        >
          {this.state.carLocations.map((carLocation, i) => (
            <MapView.Marker key={i} coordinate={carLocation}>
              <Animated.Image
                style={{
                  transform: [{ rotate: `${carLocation.rotation}deg` }],
                }}
                source={require('../img/car.png')}
              />
            </MapView.Marker>
          ))}
        </MapView>
      </View>
    );
  }
}

...
```

We have added an array of `carLocations` to be shown on the map as markers. Inside our `render` function, we will iterate over this array and place the corresponding `<MapView.Marker/>` in the provided coordinates. Inside each marker, we will add the image of the car rotating it by a specific number of degrees, so they match the streets directions. Rotating images must be done with the `Animated` API, which will be better explained later in this chapter.

Let's add a new property in our state to store a human-readable position for the location in which the map is centered:

```
/** * src/main.js ** */

import GeoCoder from 'react-native-geocoder';

export default class Main extends React.Component {
  constructor(props) {
    super(props);
    this.state = {
      position: null,

      ...

    };

    ...

  }

  _onRegionChange(region) {
    this.setState({ position: null });
    const self = this;
    if (this.timeoutId) clearTimeout(this.timeoutId);
    this.timeoutId = setTimeout(async () => {
      try {
        const res = await GeoCoder.geocodePosition({
          lat: region.latitude,
          lng: region.longitude,
        });
        self.setState({ position: res[0] });
      } catch (err) {
        console.log(err);
      }
    }, 2000);
  }
  componentDidMount() {
    this._onRegionChange.call(this, this.initialRegion);
  }

  render() {
    <View style={{ flex: 1 }}>
      <MapView
        style={styles.fullScreenMap}
        initialRegion={this.initialRegion}
        onRegionChange={this._onRegionChange.bind(this)}
      >
```

```
    . . .

      </MapView>
    </View>;
  }
}

  . . .
```

To fill this state variable, we also created a function _onRegionChange, which uses the react-native-geocoder module. This module uses Google Maps reverse geocoding services to translate some coordinates into a human-readable location. Because it's a Google Service, we might need to add an API key in order to authenticate our app with the service. All the instructions to get this module fully installed can be found at its repository URL https://github.com/airbnb/react-native-maps/blob/master/docs/installation.md.

We want this state variable to be available from the first mount of the main component, so we will call _onRegionChange in componentDidMount so that the name of the initial location is also stored in the state. Moreover, we will add the onRegionChange property on our <MapView/> to ensure the name of the location is recalculated every time the map is moved to show a different region, so we always have the name of the location in the center of the map in our position state variable.

As a final step on this screen, we will add all the subviews and another function to confirm the booking request:

```
/** * src/main.js ** */

. . .

import LocationPin from './components/LocationPin';
import LocationSearch from './components/LocationSearch';
import ClassSelection from './components/ClassSelection';
import ConfirmationModal from './components/ConfirmationModal';

export default class Main extends React.Component {
  . . .

  _onBookingRequest() {
    this.setState({
      confirmationModalVisible: true,
    });
  }

  render() {
```

```
    return (
      <View style={{ flex: 1 }}>
        ...

        <LocationSearch
          value={
            this.state.position &&
            (this.state.position.feature ||
              this.state.position.formattedAddress)
          }
        />
        <LocationPin onPress={this._onBookingRequest.bind(this)} />
        <ClassSelection />
        <ConfirmationModal
          visible={this.state.confirmationModalVisible}
          onClose={() => {
            this.setState({ confirmationModalVisible: false });
          }}
        />
      </View>
    );
  }
}

  ...
```

We added four subviews:

- LocationSearch: The component in which we will show the user the location that is centered on the map so she can know the name of the location she is exactly requesting the pickup.
- LocationPin: A pinpointing to the center of the map, so the user can see on the map where she will request the pickup. It will also display a button to confirm the pickup.
- ClassSelection: A bar where the user can select the type of car for the pickup (economy, special, or superior).
- ConfirmationModal: The modal displaying the confirmation of the request.

The _onBookingRequest method will be responsible for bringing the confirmation modal up when a booking is requested.

Adding images to our app

React Native deals with images in a similar way as websites do: images should be placed in a folder inside the projects folder structure, and then they can be referenced from the `<Image />` (or `<Animated.Image />>`) by the `source` property. Let's see an example from our app:

- `car.png`: This is placed inside the `img/` folder in the root of our project
- Then the image will be displayed by creating an `<Image/>` component using the `source` property:

  ```
  <Image source={require('../img/car.png')} />
  ```

  Notice how the `source` property doesn't accept a string, but a `require('../img/car.png')`. This is a special case in React Native and may change in future versions.

LocationSearch

This should be a simple textbox displaying the human-readable name of the location in which the map is centered. Let's take a look at the code:

```
/*** src/components/LocationSearch.js ** */

import React from 'react';
import {
  View,
  Text,
  TextInput,
  ActivityIndicator,
  StyleSheet,
} from 'react-native';

export default class LocationSearch extends React.Component {
  render() {
    return (
      <View style={styles.container}>
        <Text style={styles.title}>PICKUP LOCATION</Text>
        {this.props.value && (
          <TextInput style={styles.location} value={this.props.value} />
        )}
        {!this.props.value && <ActivityIndicator style={styles.spinner} />}
      </View>
    );
```

```
    }
  }

  const styles = StyleSheet.create({
    container: {
      backgroundColor: 'white',
      margin: 20,
      marginTop: 40,
      height: 60,
      padding: 10,
      borderColor: '#ccc',
      borderWidth: 1,
    },
    title: {
      alignSelf: 'center',
      fontSize: 12,
      color: 'green',
      fontWeight: 'bold',
    },
    location: {
      height: 40,
      textAlign: 'center',
      fontSize: 13,
    },
    spinner: {
      margin: 10,
    },
  });
```

It receives only one property: `value` (the name of the location to be displayed). If it's not set, it will display a spinner to show activity.

Because there are many different styles to be applied in this component, it's beneficial to use the `StyleSheet` API to organize the styles in a key/value object and refer it from our `render` method. This separation between logic and style helps in readability of the code and also enables code reuse as the styles can be cascaded down to child components.

Aligning elements

React Native uses Flexbox for setting up the layout of the elements in an app. This is mostly straightforward, but sometimes it can be confusing when it comes to aligning elements as there are four properties that can be used for this purpose:

- `justifyContent`: It defines the alignment of the child elements through the main axis

- `alignItems`: It defines the alignment of the child elements through the cross-axis
- `alignContent`: It aligns a flex container's lines within when there is extra space in the cross-axis
- `alignSelf`: It allows the default alignment (or the one specified by `alignItems`) to be overridden for individual flex items

The first three properties should be assigned to the container element, while the fourth one will be applied to a child element in case we want to override the default alignment.

In our case, we only want one element (the title) to be center aligned so we can use `alignSelf: 'center'`. Later in this chapter, we will see other uses for the different `align` properties.

LocationPin

In this section, we will focus on building the pinpointing to the center of the map to visually confirm the pickup location. This pin also contains a button, which can be used to trigger a pickup request:

```
/** * src/components/LocationPin.js ** */

import React from 'react';
import {
  View,
  Text,
  Dimensions,
  TouchableOpacity,
  StyleSheet,
} from 'react-native';

const { height, width } = Dimensions.get('window');

export default class LocationPin extends React.Component {
  render() {
    return (
      <View style={styles.container}>
        <View style={styles.banner}>
          <Text style={styles.bannerText}>SET PICKUP LOCATION</Text>
          <TouchableOpacity
            style={styles.bannerButton}
            onPress={this.props.onPress}
          >
            <Text style={styles.bannerButtonText}>{'>'}</Text>
```

```
                    </TouchableOpacity>
                </View>
                <View style={styles.bannerPole} />
            </View>
        );
    }
}

const styles = StyleSheet.create({
    container: {
        position: 'absolute',
        top: height / 2 - 60,
        left: width / 2 - 120,
    },
    banner: {
        flexDirection: 'row',
        alignSelf: 'center',
        justifyContent: 'center',
        borderRadius: 20,
        backgroundColor: '#333',
        padding: 10,
        paddingBottom: 10,
        shadowColor: '#000000',
        shadowOffset: {
            width: 0,
            height: 3,
        },
        shadowRadius: 5,
        shadowOpacity: 1.0,
    },
    bannerText: {
        alignSelf: 'center',
        color: 'white',
        marginRight: 10,
        marginLeft: 10,
        fontSize: 18,
    },
    bannerButton: {
        borderWidth: 1,
        borderColor: '#ccc',
        width: 26,
        height: 26,
        borderRadius: 13,
    },
    bannerButtonText: {
        color: 'white',
        textAlign: 'center',
        backgroundColor: 'transparent',
```

```
      fontSize: 18,
   },
   bannerPole: {
      backgroundColor: '#333',
      width: 3,
      height: 30,
      alignSelf: 'center',
   },
});
```

This component is again very light in terms of functionality, but has a lot of custom style. Let's dive into some of the style details.

flexDirection

By default, React Native and Flexbox stack elements vertically:

For the banner in our pin, we want to stack every element horizontally after each other as follows:

This can be achieved by adding the following styles to the containing element `flexDirection: 'row'`. The other valid options for `flexDirection` are:

- row-reverse
- `column` (default)
- `column-reverse`

Dimensions

One of the first lines of code in this component extracts the height and the width from the device into two variables:

```
const {height, width} = Dimensions.get('window');
```

Obtaining the height and width of the device enables us developers to absolute position some elements being confident they will show properly aligned. For example, we want the banner of our pin to be aligned in the center of the screen, so it points to the center of the map. We can do this by adding `{top: (height/2), left: (width/2)}` to the `banner` style in our style sheet. Of course, that would align the upper-left corner, so we need to subtract half the size of the banner to each property to ensure it gets centered in the middle of the element. This trick can be used whenever we need to align an element that is not relative to any other in the components tree although it is recommended to use relative positioning when possible.

Shadows

Let's set focus on our banner's style, specifically on the `shadows` properties:

```
banner: {
  ...
  shadowColor: '#000000',
  shadowOffset: {
    width: 0,
    height: 3
  },
  shadowRadius: 5,
  shadowOpacity: 1.0
}
```

In order to add a shadow to a component, we need to add four properties:

- `shadowColor`: This adds the hexadecimal or RGBA value of the color we want for our component
- `shadowOffset`: This shows how far we want our shadow to be casted
- `shadowRadius`: This shows the value of the radius in the corner of our shadow
- `shadowOpacity`: This shows how dark we want our shadow to be

That's it for our `LocationPin` component.

ClassSelection

In this component, we will explore the `Animated` API in React Native to get started with animations. Moreover, we will use custom fonts to improve the user experience and increase the feeling of customization in our app:

```
/*** src/components/ClassSelection.js ** */

import React from 'react';
import {
  View,
  Image,
  Dimensions,
  Text,
  TouchableOpacity,
  Animated,
  StyleSheet,
} from 'react-native';

const { height, width } = Dimensions.get('window');

export default class ClassSelection extends React.Component {
  constructor(props) {
    super(props);
    this.state = {
      classButtonPosition: new Animated.Value(15 + width * 0.1),
    };
  }

  _onClassChange(className) {
    if (className === 'superior') {
      Animated.timing(this.state.classButtonPosition, {
        toValue: width * 0.77,
        duration: 500,
      }).start();
    }

    if (className === 'special') {
      Animated.timing(this.state.classButtonPosition, {
        toValue: width * 0.5 - 20,
        duration: 500,
      }).start();
    }

    if (className === 'economy') {
      Animated.timing(this.state.classButtonPosition, {
        toValue: 15 + width * 0.1,
```

```
            duration: 500,
        }).start();
    }
}

    render() {
        return (
            <View style={styles.container}>
                <Image
                    style={styles.classBar}
                    source={require('../../img/classBar.png')}
                />
                <Animated.View
                    style={{[styles.classButton, { left:
this.state.classButtonPosition }]}
                >
                    <Image
                        style={styles.classButtonImage}
                        source={require('../../img/class.png')}
                    />
                </Animated.View>
                <TouchableOpacity
                    style={[
                        styles.classButtonContainer,
                        {
                            width: width / 3 - 10,
                            left: width * 0.11,
                        },
                    ]}
                    onPress={this._onClassChange.bind(this, 'economy')}
                >
                    <Text style={styles.classLabel}>economy</Text>
                </TouchableOpacity>
                <TouchableOpacity
                    style={[
                        styles.classButtonContainer,
                        { width: width / 3, left: width / 3 },
                    ]}
                    onPress={this._onClassChange.bind(this, 'special')}
                >
                    <Text style={[styles.classLabel, { textAlign: 'center' }]}>
                        Special
                    </Text>
                </TouchableOpacity>
                <TouchableOpacity
                    style={[
                        styles.classButtonContainer,
                        { width: width / 3, right: width * 0.11 },
```

```
        ]}
        onPress={this._onClassChange.bind(this, 'superior')}
      >
        <Text style={[styles.classLabel, { textAlign: 'right' }]}>
          Superior
        </Text>
      </TouchableOpacity>
    </View>
  );
  }
}

const styles = StyleSheet.create({
  container: {
    height: 80,
    backgroundColor: 'white',
    position: 'absolute',
    bottom: 0,
    left: 0,
    right: 0,
    paddingBottom: 10,
  },
  classBar: {
    width: width * 0.7,
    left: width * 0.15,
    resizeMode: 'contain',
    height: 30,
    top: 35,
  },
  classButton: {
    top: 30,
    justifyContent: 'center',
    borderRadius: 20,
    borderColor: '#ccc',
    borderWidth: 1,
    position: 'absolute',
    backgroundColor: 'white',
    height: 40,
    width: 40,
  },
  classButtonImage: {
    alignSelf: 'center',
    resizeMode: 'contain',
    width: 30,
  },
  classButtonContainer: {
    backgroundColor: 'transparent',
    position: 'absolute',
```

```
      height: 70,
      top: 10,
    },
    classLabel: {
      paddingTop: 5,
      fontSize: 12,
    },
  });
```

This simple component is made out of five sub components:

- `classBar`: This is an image showing the bar and the stop points for each class
- `classButton`: This is the round button, which will be moved to the selected class once the user presses a specific class
- `classButtonContainer`: This is the touchable component detecting what class the user wants to select
- `classLabel`: These are titles for each class to be displayed on top of the bar

Let's start by taking a look at the styles as we can find a new property for image components: `resizeMode`, which determines how to resize the image when the frame doesn't match the raw image dimensions. From the five possible values (`cover`, `contain`, `stretch`, `repeat`, and `center`), we chose `contain` as we want to scale the image uniformly (maintain the image's aspect ratio) so that both dimensions of the image will be equal to or less than the corresponding dimension of the view. We are using these properties both in `classBar` and `classButtonImage` being the two images we will need to resize in this view.

Adding custom fonts

React Native includes a long list of cross-platform fonts available by default. The list of fonts can be checked on `https://github.com/react-native-training/react-native-fonts`.

Nevertheless, adding custom fonts is a common need when developing apps, especially when designers are involved, so we will use our car booking app as a playground to test this functionality.

Adding custom fonts to our app is a three steps task:

1. Add the font file (.ttf) into a folder inside our project. We used fonts/ for this app.

2. Add the following lines to our package.json:

```
"rnpm": {
    "assets": ["./fonts"]
}
```

3. Run the following command in a terminal:

```
react-native link
```

That's it, React Native's CLI will handle the insertion of the fonts folder and its files inside the iOS and Android project at once. Our fonts will be available by their font name (which may not be the same as the filename). In our case, we have fontFamily: 'Blair ITC' in our style sheet.

We can now modify our classLabel style in the ClassSelection component to include the new font:

```
. . .

classLabel: {
    fontFamily: 'Blair ITC',
    paddingTop: 5,
    fontSize: 12,
},

. . .
```

Animations

React Native's Animated API is designed to make it very easy to concisely express a wide variety of interesting animation and interaction patterns in a very performant way. Animated focuses on declarative relationships between inputs and outputs, with configurable transforms in between, and simple start/stop methods to control time-based animation execution.

What we want to do in our app is to move the `classButton` to a specific location whenever the user presses the class she wants to book. Let's take a closer look at how we are using this API in our app:

```
/** * src/components/ClassSelection ***/

...

export default class ClassSelection extends React.Component {
  constructor(props) {
    super(props);
    this.state = {
      classButtonPosition: new Animated.Value(15 + width * 0.1),
    };
  }

  _onClassChange(className) {
    if (className === 'superior') {
      Animated.timing(this.state.classButtonPosition, {
        toValue: width * 0.77,
        duration: 500,
      }).start();
    }

    ...

  }

  render() {
    return (
      ...

      <Animated.View style={{ left: this.state.classButtonPosition }}>
        <Image
          style={styles.classButtonImage}
          source={require('../../img/class.png')}
        />
      </Animated.View>

      ...

      <TouchableOpacity
        onPress={this._onClassChange.bind(this, 'superior')}
      >
        <Text>Superior</Text>
      </TouchableOpacity>

      ...
```

```
    );
   }
  }

 ...
```

For this movement to happen correctly, we need to wrap the `classButtonImage` in `Animated.View` and provide an initial `Animated.Value` to it as a left coordinate. We will use `this.state.classButtonPosition` for this matter so that we can change it when the user selects a specific class.

We are ready to start our animation. It will be triggered by the `_onClassChange` method, as it is the one invoked when the user presses `classButtonContainer` (`<TouchableOpacity/>`). This method is calling the `Animated.timing` function passing two parameters:

- The animated value to drive (`this.state.classButtonPosition`)
- An object containing the end value and the duration of the animation

Invoking `Animated.timing` will result in an object containing the `start()` method, which we call right away to start the animation. React Native will then know that the `left` coordinate of the `Animated.View` needs to be slowly changed according to the provided parameters.

As this may feel a bit overcomplicated for a simple move animation, it allows a wide range of customization as chaining animations or modifying the easing functions. We will see a rotation animation later in this chapter.

ConfirmationModal

Our last component is a modal view, which will be opened once the user has pressed on the **SET PICKUP LOCATION** button on the location pin. We will display the modal and a custom activity indicator, which will use a complex animation setup to continuously rotate in its position:

```
/** * src/components/ConfirmationModal.js ***/

import React from 'react';
import {
  Modal,
  View,
  Text,
  Animated,
```

```
  Easing,
  TouchableOpacity,
  StyleSheet,
} from 'react-native';

export default class ConfirmationModal extends React.Component {
  componentWillMount() {
    this._animatedValue = new Animated.Value(0);
  }

  cycleAnimation() {
    Animated.sequence([
      Animated.timing(this._animatedValue, {
        toValue: 100,
        duration: 1000,
        easing: Easing.linear,
      }),
      Animated.timing(this._animatedValue, {
        toValue: 0,
        duration: 0,
      }),
    ]).start(() => {
      this.cycleAnimation();
    });
  }

  componentDidMount() {
    this.cycleAnimation();
  }

  render() {
    const interpolatedRotateAnimation = this._animatedValue.interpolate({
      inputRange: [0, 100],
      outputRange: ['0deg', '360deg'],
    });

    return (
      <Modal
        animationType={'fade'}
        visible={this.props.visible}
        transparent={true}
      >
        <View style={styles.overlay}>
          <View style={styles.container}>
            <Text style={styles.title}>Contacting nearest car...</Text>
            <Animated.Image
              style={[
                styles.spinner,
```

```
            { transform: [{ rotate: interpolatedRotateAnimation }] },
          ]}
          source={require('../../img/loading.png')}
        />
        <TouchableOpacity
          style={styles.closeButton}
          onPress={this.props.onClose}
        >
          <Text style={styles.closeButtonText}>X</Text>
        </TouchableOpacity>
      </View>
    </View>
  </Modal>
      );
  }
}

const styles = StyleSheet.create({
  overlay: {
    flex: 1,
    backgroundColor: '#0006',
    justifyContent: 'center',
  },
  container: {
    backgroundColor: 'white',
    alignSelf: 'center',
    padding: 20,
    borderColor: '#ccc',
    borderWidth: 1,
  },
  title: {
    textAlign: 'right',
    fontFamily: 'Blair ITC',
    paddingTop: 5,
    fontSize: 12,
  },
  spinner: {
    resizeMode: 'contain',
    height: 50,
    width: 50,
    margin: 50,
    alignSelf: 'center',
  },
  closeButton: {
    backgroundColor: '#333',
    width: 40,
    height: 40,
    borderRadius: 20,
```

```
      justifyContent: 'center',
      alignSelf: 'center',
   },
   closeButtonText: {
      color: 'white',
      alignSelf: 'center',
      fontSize: 20,
   },
});
```

For this component, we are using the `<Modal />` component available in React Native to take advantage of its fade animation and visibility capabilities. The property `this.props.visible` will drive the visibility of this component as it is the parent who is aware of the pickup request from the user.

Let's focus again on animations as we want to do a more complex setup for the spinner showing activity. We want to display an endless rotating animation, so we need to systematically call our `start()` animation method. In order to achieve this, we created a `cycleAnimation()` method, which is called on the component mount (to get the animation started) and from the `Animated.timing` returned object as it is passed as a callback to be invoked every time the animation ends.

We are also using `Animated.sequence` to concatenate two animations:

- Moving from 0 degrees to 360 (in one second using a linear easing)
- Moving from 360 degrees to 0 (in 0 seconds)

This is required to repeat the first animation over at the end of each cycle.

Finally, we defined a variable named `interpolatedRotateAnimation` to store the interpolation from 0 degrees to 360, so it can be passed to the `transform/rotate` style defining what are going to be the available rotation values when animating our `Animated.Image`.

As an experiment, we can try and change loading.png with an alternative image and see how it gets animated. This can be easily achieved by replacing the source prop in our <Animated.Image /> component:

```
   ...

         <Animated.Image
           style={[
             styles.spinner,
             { transform: [{ rotate: interpolatedRotateAnimation }] },
           ]}
```

```
    source={require('../../img/spinner.png')}
/>
```

. . .

Summary

Using UI libraries such as `native-base` or `react-native-elements` saves a lot of time and maintenance hassle when we need to build apps, but the results end up having a standard flavor, which is not always desirable in terms of user experience. That's why learning how to manipulate the style of our apps is always a good idea, especially on teams where the design is provided by UX specialists or app designers.

In this chapter, we took a deep look into the folders and files created by React Native's CLI when initializing a project. Moreover, we familiarized ourselves with the developer menu and its debugging functionalities.
When building our app we set the focus on the layouts and component styling, but also on how to add and manipulate animations to make our interface more appealing to the user. We took a look at Flexbox layout system and how to stack and center elements in our components. API's such as dimensions were used to retrieve the device width and height to perform positioning tricks on some components.
You learned how to add fonts and images into our app and how to show them to improve the user experience.

Now that we know how to build more custom interfaces, let's build in the next chapter an image sharing app in which design plays a key role.

4
Image Sharing App

At this point, we know how to create a fully-featured app with a custom interface. You even learned how to add a state management library to control shared data in our app so that the code base remains maintainable and scalable.

In this chapter, we will focus on building the app with a different state management library (Redux), using the camera capabilities, writing platform-specific code, and diving deeper into building a custom user interface, which is both appealing and usable. An image sharing app will serve as a good example for these features and also will set up the basis for understanding how big apps should be built on React Native.

We will reuse most of our code for the two platforms where this app will be available: iOS and Android. Although most of our user interface will be custom, we will use `native-base` to simplify UI elements as icons. For navigation, we will use `react-navigation` again as it provides the most commonly used navigation for each platform: tabbed navigation for iOS and drawer menu navigation for Android. Finally, we will use `react-native-camera` to handle the interaction with the device's camera. This will not only reduce implementation complexity but also will provide us with a large set of features for free that we could use to extend our app in the future.

For this app, we will mock up a number of API calls so that we don't need to build a backend. These calls should be easily replaced by real API when the time to build a connected app comes.

Overview

One of the main requirements when building an image sharing app is an appealing design. We will follow the design patterns for some of the most popular image sharing apps, adapting those patterns for each platform while trying to reuse as much code as possible taking advantage of React Native's cross-platform capabilities.

Let's first take a look at the user interface in iOS:

The main screen shows a simple header and a list of images, including the user picture, name, and a **More** icon to share the image. At the bottom, the tabbed navigation displays three icons representing the three main screens: **All Images**, **My Images**, and **Camera**.

All images used for this sample app are free to be used in any form.

When a user presses the **More** icon for a specific image, the **Share** menu will be displayed:

This is a standard iOS component. It doesn't make much sense to use it on a simulator, it can be better tested on an actual device.

Let's take a look at the second screen, **My Images**:

This is a grid representation of all the images uploaded by the current user, which can be updated by the next screen, **Camera**:

The iOS simulator doesn't include support for any camera, so this feature is again better tested on an actual device, although `react-native-camera` is fully usable and will return fake data when accessed. We will use a static image for testing purposes.

That's all for iOS; let's move now to the Android version:

As Android encourages drawer-based navigation instead of tabs, we will include a drawer menu icon in the header and will also make the camera available through a different icon.

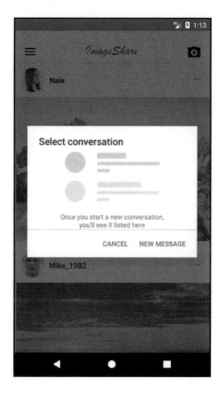

As with the iOS **Share** menu, Android has its own controller, so we will take advantage of this feature and include it whenever a user taps on the **More** icon on a specific image:

When a user taps on the drawer menu icon, the menu will be displayed, revealing the three available screens. From here, the user can navigate to the **My Images** screen:

Finally, the camera screen will also be accessible through the drawer menu:

The Android Simulator includes a camera simulation consisting of a colored moving square, which can be used for testing. Instead, we will stick with the fixed image we used in the iOS version for consistency reasons.

We will be covering the following topics in this chapter:

- Redux in React Native
- Using the camera
- Platform-specific code
- Drawer and tabbed navigation
- Sharing data with other apps

Setting up the folder structure

Let's initialize a React Native project using React Native's CLI. The project will be named imageShare and will be available for iOS and Android devices:

```
react-native init --version="0.44.0" imageShare
```

In order to use some packages in this app, we will be using a specific version of React Native (0.44.0).

We will be using Redux for our app, so we will create a folder structure in which we can accommodate our `reducers`, `actions`, `components`, `screens`, and `api` calls:

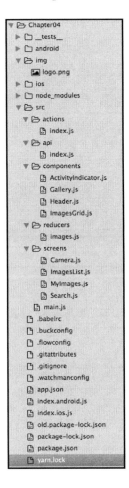

Moreover, we have added `logo.png` in the `img` folder. For the rest, we have a very standard React Native project. The entry point will be `index.ios.js` for iOS and `index.android.js` for Android:

```
/*** index.ios.js and index.android.js ***/

import { AppRegistry } from 'react-native';
import App from './src/main';

AppRegistry.registerComponent('imageShare', () => App);
```

We have the same implementation for both files as we want to use `src/main.js` as the common entry point for both platforms.

Let's jump into our `package.json` file to understand which dependencies we will have in our app:

```
/*** package.json ***/

{
        "name": "imageShare",
        "version": "0.0.1",
        "private": true,
        "scripts": {
                "start": "node node_modules/react-native/
                local-cli/cli.js start",
                "test": "jest"
        },
        "dependencies": {
                "native-base": "^2.1.5",
                "react": "16.0.0-alpha.6",
                "react-native": "0.44.0",
                "react-native-camera": "^0.8.0",
                "react-navigation": "^1.0.0-beta.9",
                "react-redux": "^5.0.5",
                "redux": "^3.6.0",
                "redux-thunk": "^2.2.0"
        },
        "devDependencies": {
                "babel-jest": "20.0.3",
                "babel-preset-react-native": "1.9.2",
                "jest": "20.0.3",
                "react-test-renderer": "16.0.0-alpha.6"
        },
        "jest": {
                "preset": "react-native"
        }
}
```

Some of the dependencies, such as `react-navigation` or `native-base`, are old acquaintances from previous chapters. Others, such as `react-native-camera`, will be introduced in this chapter for the first time. Some of them are closely related to the state management library we will be using for this app, Redux:

- `redux`: This is the state management library itself
- `react-redux`: These are the React handlers for Redux

- `redux-thunk`: This is Redux middleware that handles asynchronous action execution

To complete the installation, we will need to link `react-native-camera` as it requires some changes in the native part of our app:

```
react-native link react-native-camera
```

On iOS 10 and higher, we also need to modify our `ios/imageShare/Info.plist` to add a *Camera Usage Description*, which should be displayed to request permission to enable the camera within the app. We need to add these lines right before the last `</dict></plist>`:

```
<key>NSCameraUsageDescription</key>
<string>imageShare requires access to the camera on this device to perform
this action</string>
<key>NSPhotoLibraryUsageDescription</key>
<string>imageShare requires access to the image library on this device to
perform this action</string>
```

Redux

Redux is a predictable state container for JavaScript apps based on simple principles:

- The whole state of your app is stored in an object tree inside a single *store*
- The only way to change the state tree is to emit an *action*, an object describing what happened
- To specify how the actions transform the state tree, you write pure *reducers*

Its popularity comes from the degree of consistency, testability, and developer experience that can be derived from its use in any kind of code base (frontend or backend). It's also simple to reason and master due to its strict unidirectional data flow:

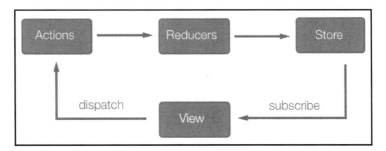

User triggers and **Actions** that are processed by **Reducers**, which are just pure functions applying changes to the state based on that **Action**. The resulting state is saved in a single **Store**, which is used by the **View** in our app to display the current state of the application.

Redux is a complex topic that falls out of the scope of this book, but it will be extensively used throughout some of the chapters in this book, so it could be beneficial to take a look at their official documentation (`http://redux.js.org/`) to get acquainted with the basic concepts of this state management library.

Some of the basic concepts of Redux will be used in our `src/main.js` file:

```
/*** src/main.js ***/

import React from 'react';
import { DrawerNavigator, TabNavigator } from 'react-navigation';
import { Platform } from 'react-native';

import { Provider } from 'react-redux';
import { createStore, combineReducers, applyMiddleware } from 'redux';
import thunk from 'redux-thunk';
import imagesReducer from './reducers/images';

import ImagesList from './screens/ImagesList.js';
import MyImages from './screens/MyImages.js';
import Camera from './screens/Camera.js';

let Navigator;
if(Platform.OS === 'ios'){
  Navigator = TabNavigator({
    ImagesList: { screen: ImagesList },
    MyImages: { screen: MyImages },
    Camera: { screen: Camera }
  }, {
    tabBarOptions: {
      inactiveTintColor: '#aaa',
      activeTintColor: '#000',
      showLabel: false
    }
  });
} else {
  Navigator = DrawerNavigator({
    ImagesList: { screen: ImagesList },
    MyImages: { screen: MyImages },
    Camera: { screen: Camera }
  });
}
```

```
let store = createStore(combineReducers({ imagesReducer }),
applyMiddleware(thunk));

export default class App extends React.Component {
  render() {
    return (
      <Provider store={store}>
        <Navigator/>
      </Provider>
    )
  }
}
```

Let's focus first on the Redux ceremony. `let store = createStore(combineReducers({ imagesReducer }), applyMiddleware(thunk));` sets up the store by combining the imported reducers (we only have one reducer for this app, so this is merely informative) and applying the *Thunk* middleware, which will enable our app to use asynchronous actions. We will simulate several API calls that will return asynchronous promises, so this middleware is needed to properly handle the resolutions of those promises.

Then, we have our `render` method:

```
<Provider store={store}>
  <Navigator/>
</Provider>
```

This is standard in most Redux apps using React. We wrap the root component (`<Navigator />` in our case) with a `<Provider />` component to ensure that we will have the `store` available from the root of our app. The Redux `connect` method will be available for us to use in our containers or screens as we proceed in this chapter.

We will use a `<Navigator />` component as the root of our app, but it will have a different nature based on which platform is running:

```
let Navigator;
if(Platform.OS === 'ios'){
  Navigator = TabNavigator({

    ...

  });
} else {
  Navigator = DrawerNavigator({

    ...

  });
}
```

`Platform` is a React Native API used mainly to identify which platform our app is running on. We can write iOS-specific code by enclosing that code with `if(Platform.OS === 'ios'){ ... }` and the same goes for Android: `if(Platform.OS === 'android'){ ... }`.

In this case, we are using it to build a tabbed navigator on iOS and a drawer navigator on Android, which are the *de facto* navigation patterns for those platforms. On both navigators, we will set `ImagesList`, `MyImages`, and `Camera` as the three main screens in our app.

ImagesList

The main screen in our app is a list of images retrieved from the backend. We will display this images together with their corresponding uploader profile pictures and names. For each image, we will show **More**, which can be used to share the image with other apps on the user's device, such as messaging apps or social networks. Most of the UI for this screen will be derived from the `<Gallery />` component, so we will focus on connecting the screen with Redux store, adding a custom header, and a scroll view to make the gallery scrollable, and adding an activity indicator to warn the user about network activity:

```
/*** src/components/ImagesList ***/

import React from 'react';
import { View, ScrollView } from 'react-native';

import { bindActionCreators } from 'redux';
import { connect } from 'react-redux';
import * as Actions from '../actions';
import { Icon } from 'native-base';

import Header from '../components/Header';
import Gallery from '../components/Gallery';
import ActivityIndicator from '../components/ActivityIndicator';

class ImagesList extends React.Component {
  static navigationOptions = {
    tabBarIcon: ({ tintColor }) => (
      <Icon name='list' style={{fontSize: 40, color: tintColor}}/>
    ),
    drawerLabel: 'All Images'
  };

  componentWillMount() {
    this.props.fetchImages();
  }
```

```
componentWillReceiveProps(nextProps) {
  if(!this.props.addingImage && nextProps.addingImage) {
    this.scrollable.scrollTo({y: 0});
  }
}

render() {
  return (
    <View style={{flex: 1}}>
      <Header onMenuButtonPress={() =>
      this.props.navigation.navigate('DrawerOpen')}
      onCameraButtonPress={() =>
      this.props.navigation.navigate('Camera')}/>
      <ScrollView ref={(scrollable) => {
          this.scrollable = scrollable;
        }}>
        { this.props.addingImage && <ActivityIndicator
          message='Adding image' /> }
        <Gallery imageList={this.props.images} loading=
        {this.props.fetchingImages}/>
      </ScrollView>
    </View>
  );
}
}

function mapStateToProps(state) { return { images:
state.imagesReducer.images, addingImage: state.imagesReducer.addingImage,
fetchingImages: state.imagesReducer.fetchingImages } }
function mapStateActionsToProps(dispatch) { return
bindActionCreators(Actions, dispatch) }

export default connect(mapStateToProps,
mapStateActionsToProps)(ImagesList);
```

As most of the React apps use Redux, we need to connect our component with the state and the actions. We will create two functions (mapStateToProps and mapStateActionsToProps) to decorate our <ImageList /> component with the mapped actions and parts of the state the component is interested in:

- images: This is the list of images we will use to render in our <Gallery />
- addingImage: This is a flag we will set to true when uploading an image
- fetchingImages: This is a flag that will be set to true when the app requests the list of images to the backend in order to update the store

The only action we will need on this screen is fetchImages, which is accessible through the props component because we connected the list of actions in Actions to our <ImagesList /> component. On a similar note, we have the three state variables (images, addingImage, and fetchingImages) available through props, thanks to the same connect invocation:

```
function mapStateToProps(state) {
  return {
    images: state.imagesReducer.images,
    addingImage: state.imagesReducer.addingImage,
    fetchingImages: state.imagesReducer.fetchingImages
  };
}
function mapStateActionsToProps(dispatch) {
  return bindActionCreators(Actions, dispatch);
}

export default connect(mapStateToProps,
mapStateActionsToProps)(ImagesList);
```

That's all we need from Redux. We will see this pattern in other screens as well, as it's a common solution for connecting React components with parts of the store and the list of actions.

The fetchImages action is called on componentWillMount as the initial retrieval of the list of images to be rendered:

```
componentWillMount() {
  this.props.fetchImages();
}
```

We also added a way to detect the moment the addingImage flag is set to true to display the activity indicator:

```
componentWillReceiveProps(nextProps) {
  if(!this.props.addingImage && nextProps.addingImage) {
    this.scrollable.scrollTo({y: 0});
  }
}
```

This method will call scrollTo in the <Scrollview /> to make sure it displays the top part, so the <ActivityIndicator /> is visible to the user. We are using a custom <ActivityIndicator /> this time (imported from src/components/ActivityIndicator), as we want to display not only a spinner but also a message.

Last, we will add two components:

- `<Header />`: This displays the logo and (in the Android version) two icons to navigate to the drawer menu and the camera screen

- `<Gallery />`: This shows the formatted list of images and uploaders

Before moving to another screen, let's take a look at the three custom components we included in this one: `<ActivityIndicator />`, `<Header />`, and `<Gallery />`.

Gallery

Gallery holds all the rendering logic for the list of images. It relies on `native-base` and, more specifically, on two of its components, `<List />` and `<ListItem />`:

```
/*** src/components/Gallery ***/

import React from 'react';
import { List, ListItem, Text, Icon, Button, Container, Content }
 from 'native-base';
import { Image, Dimensions, View, Share, ActivityIndicator, StyleSheet }
from 'react-native';

var {height, width} = Dimensions.get('window');

export default class Gallery extends React.Component {
  _share(image) {
   Share.share({message: image.src, title: 'Image from: ' +
               image.user.name})
  }

  render() {
    return (
      <View>
        <List style={{margin: -15}}>
          {
            this.props.imageList && this.props.imageList.map((image) =>
            {
              return (
                <ListItem
                   key={image.id}
                   style={{borderBottomWidth: 0,
                   flexDirection: 'column', marginBottom: -20}}>
                 <View style={styles.user}>
```

```
                    <Image source={{uri: image.user.pic}}
                     style={styles.userPic}/>
                    <Text style={{fontWeight: 'bold'}}>
                    {image.user.name}</Text>
                  </View>
                  <Image source={{uri: image.src}}
                  style={styles.image}/>
                  <Button style={{position: 'absolute', right: 15,
                  top: 25}} transparent
                  onPress={this._share.bind(this, image)}>
                    <Icon name='ios-more' style={{fontSize: 20,
                    color: 'black'}}/>
                  </Button>
                </ListItem>
              );
            })
          }
        </List>
        {
          this.props.loading &&
          <View style={styles.spinnerContainer}>
            <ActivityIndicator/>
          </View>
        }
      </View>
    );
  }
}

const styles = StyleSheet.create({
  user: {
    flexDirection: 'row',
    alignSelf: 'flex-start',
    padding: 10
  },
  userPic: {
    width: 50,
    height: 50,
    resizeMode: 'cover',
    marginRight: 10,
    borderRadius: 25
  },
  image: {
    width: width,
    height: 300,
    resizeMode: 'cover'
  },
  spinnerContainer: {
```

```
      justifyContent: 'center',
      height: (height - 50)
   }
});
```

This component takes two props from its parent: `loading` and `imageList`.

`loading` is used to display a standard `<ActivityIndicator />` showing the user network activity. This time we are using the standard one instead of a custom indicator as it should be clear enough what the network activity is indicating.

`imageList` is the array storing the list of images, which will be rendered in our `<Gallery />` one `<ListenItem />` at a time. Each `<ListItem />` holds a `<Button />` with `onPress={this._share.bind(this, image)` to share the image with other apps. Let's take a look at the `_share` function:

```
_share(image) {
   Share.share({message: image.src, title: 'Image from: '
                + image.user.name})
}
```

`Share` is a React Native API for sharing text content. In our case, we will share the URL (`img.src`) of the image together with a simple title. Sharing text is the easiest way of sharing content between apps, as many apps would accept text as a shared format.

It's also worth noting the style we apply to the image to take over the whole width and a fixed height (`300`), so we have a stable layout for all images even when the display images have different sizes. For this setup, we use `resizeMode: 'cover'` so the images are not stretched in any dimension. This means we may end up cutting the image, but it compensates on uniformity. Another option would be to use `resizeMode: contain` if we don't want to cut anything, but rather want to fit the image inside these bounds while possibly shrinking them.

Header

We want to reuse a custom header between several screens. That's why it's best to create a separate component for it and import it in those screens:

```
/*** src/components/Header ***/

import React from 'react';
import { View, Image, StyleSheet } from 'react-native';
import { Icon, Button } from 'native-base';
```

```
import { Platform } from 'react-native';

export default class Header extends React.Component {
  render() {
    return (
      <View style={styles.container}>
        {
          Platform.OS === 'android' &&
          <Button transparent onPress={this.props.onMenuButtonPress}>
            <Icon android='md-menu' style={styles.menuIcon}/>
          </Button>
        }
        <Image source={require('../../img/logo.png')}
          style={styles.logo} />
        {
          Platform.OS === 'android' &&
          <Button onPress={this.props.onCameraButtonPress} transparent>
            <Icon name='camera' style={styles.cameraIcon}/>
          </Button>
        }
      </View>
    );
  }
}

const styles = StyleSheet.create({
  container: {
    paddingTop: 20,
    flexDirection: 'row',
    alignItems: 'center',
    justifyContent: 'space-around',
    borderBottomWidth: 1,
    borderBottomColor: '#ccc'
  },
  menuIcon: {
    fontSize: 30,
    color: 'black'
  },
  logo: {
    height: 25,
    resizeMode: 'contain',
    margin: 10
  },
  cameraIcon: {
    fontSize: 30,
    color: 'black'
  }
});
```

We are using the `Platform` API again to detect Android devices and show a drawer menu button and a camera button only on that platform. We decided to do this to make those features, which are the core of the app, more prominent to Android users by reducing the number of buttons needed to be pressed to reach them. The actions to be performed when pressing the buttons are passed by the parent component through two props:

- onMenuButtonPress
- onCameraButtonPress

Those two props call two separate functions invoking the `navigate` method of the navigator:

- this.props.navigation.navigate('DrawerOpen')
- this.props.navigation.navigate('Camera')

The last thing to note is how we set up the layout for the container in this component. We use `justifyContent: 'space-around'`, which is the way we tell Flexbox to evenly distribute items in the line with equal space around them. Note that, visually, the spaces aren't equal since all the items have equal space on both sides. The first item will have one unit of space against the container edge, but two units of space between the next item because that next item has its own spacing that applies:

ActivityIndicator

Our custom `ActivityIndicator` is a very simple component:

```
/*** src/components/ActivityIndicator ***/

import React from 'react';
import { ActivityIndicator, View, Text, StyleSheet }
from 'react-native';

export default class CustomActivityIndicator extends React.Component {
  render() {
    return (
      <View style={styles.container}>
        <ActivityIndicator style={{marginRight: 10}}/>
```

```
            <Text>{this.props.message}</Text>
          </View>
      );
    }
  }

  const styles = StyleSheet.create({
    container: {
      flexDirection: 'row',
      justifyContent: 'center',
      padding: 10,
      backgroundColor: '#f0f0f0'
    }
  });
```

It receives a message as a prop and displays it next to a standard spinner. We also added a custom background color (#f0f0f0) to make it more visible over the white backgrounds.

Let's move now to the camera screen to add our images to the list.

Camera

Most of the logic when taking photos can be abstracted when using react-native-camera, so we will focus on using this module in our component and making sure we connect it to our app's state through Redux actions:

```
/*** src/screens/Camera ***/

import React, { Component } from 'react';
import {
  Dimensions,
  StyleSheet,
  Text,
  TouchableHighlight,
  View
} from 'react-native';
import { Button, Icon } from 'native-base';
import Camera from 'react-native-camera';
import { bindActionCreators } from 'redux';
import { connect } from 'react-redux';
import * as Actions from '../actions';

class CameraScreen extends Component {
  static navigationOptions = {
    tabBarIcon: ({ tintColor }) => (
```

```
        <Icon name='camera' style={{fontSize: 40, color: tintColor}}/>
      ),
    };

    render() {
      return (
        <View style={styles.container}>
          <Camera
            ref={(cam) => {
              this.camera = cam;
            }}
            style={styles.preview}
            aspect={Camera.constants.Aspect.fill}>
            <Button onPress={this.takePicture.bind(this)}
              style={styles.cameraButton} transparent>
              <Icon name='camera' style={{fontSize: 70,
              color: 'white'}}/>
            </Button>
          </Camera>
          <Button onPress={() =>
            this.props.navigation.navigate('ImagesList')}
            style={styles.backButton} transparent>
            <Icon ios='ios-arrow-dropleft' android='md-arrow-dropleft'
              style={{fontSize: 30, color: 'white'}}/>
          </Button>
        </View>
      );
    }

    takePicture() {
      const options = {};
      this.camera.capture({metadata: options})
        .then((data) => {
          this.props.addImage(data);
          this.props.navigation.navigate('ImagesList');
        })
        .catch(err => console.error(err));
    }
}

const styles = StyleSheet.create({
  container: {
    flex: 1,
    flexDirection: 'row',
  },
  preview: {
    flex: 1,
    justifyContent: 'flex-end',
```

```
      padding: 20
    },
    capture: {
      flex: 0,
      backgroundColor: '#fff',
      borderRadius: 5,
      color: '#000',
      padding: 10,
      margin: 40
    },
    cameraButton: {
      flex: 0,
      alignSelf: 'center'
    },
    backButton: {
      position: 'absolute',
      top:20
    }
});

function mapStateToProps(state) { return {} }
function mapStateActionsToProps(dispatch) { return
bindActionCreators(Actions, dispatch) }

export default connect(mapStateToProps,
mapStateActionsToProps)(CameraScreen);
```

The way `react-native-camera` works is by providing a component we can include in our screen and, through a reference, we can call its `capture` method, which returns a promise we can use to call `addImage` to upload our image to the app's backend.

Let's take a closer look at the `<Camera />` component:

```
<Camera
    ref={(cam) => {
      this.camera = cam;
    }}
    style={styles.preview}
    aspect={Camera.constants.Aspect.fill}>

...

</Camera>
```

The `<Camera />` component takes three props:

- `ref`: This sets a reference to the `<Camera />` component in the parent component for it to call the `capture` method.
- `style`: This allows the developer to specify the look of the component in the app.
- `aspect`: This allows you to define how the view renderer will behave when displaying camera's view. There are three options: `fill`, `fit`, and `stretch`.

The `takePicture` function will be invoked when the user presses the camera button:

```
takePicture() {
    const options = {};
    this.camera.capture({metadata: options})
    .then((data) => {
      this.props.addImage(data);
      this.props.navigation.navigate('ImagesList');
    })
    .catch(err => console.error(err));
}
```

We will use the saved reference to the camera to call its `capture` method to which we can pass some metadata (for example, the location in which the photo was taken). This method returns a promise, which will be resolved with the image data so we will use this data to call the `addImage` action to send this data to the backend, so the picture can be added to the `imagesList`. Right after sending the image to the backend, we will make the app navigate back to the `ImagesList` screen. The `addImage` method will set the `addingImages` flag, so the `ImageList` screen can display the activity indicator with the corresponding message.

Let's move on to the last screen in our app: `MyImages`.

MyImages

This screen shows all the images the logged user has uploaded. We are using fake images for this screen to pre-fill this screen, but more images can be added through the camera screen.

Most of the rendering logic will be moved to a separate component named `<ImagesGrid />`:

```
/*** src/screens/MyImages ***/

import React from 'react';
```

```
import {
  Image,
  TouchableOpacity,
  Text,
  View,
  ActivityIndicator,
  Dimensions
} from 'react-native';

import { bindActionCreators } from 'redux';
import { connect } from 'react-redux';
import * as Actions from '../actions';
import { Icon } from 'native-base';

import Header from '../components/Header';
import ImagesGrid from '../components/ImagesGrid';

var {height, width} = Dimensions.get('window');

class MyImages extends React.Component {
  static navigationOptions = {
    drawerLabel: 'My Images',
    tabBarIcon: ({ tintColor }) => (
      <Icon name='person' style={{fontSize: 40, color: tintColor}}/>
    )
  };

  componentWillMount() {
    this.props.fetchImages(this.props.user.name);
  }

  render() {
    return (
      <View>
        <Header onMenuButtonPress={() =>
        this.props.navigation.navigate('DrawerOpen')}
        onCameraButtonPress={() =>
        this.props.navigation.navigate('Camera')}/>
        {
          this.props.fetchingImages &&
          <View style={{justifyContent: 'center',
           height: (height - 50)}}>
            <ActivityIndicator/>
          </View>
        }
        <ImagesGrid images={this.props.images}/>
      </View>
    );
```

```
        }
    }

    function mapStateToProps(state) { return { images:
    state.imagesReducer.userImages, user: state.imagesReducer.user,
    fetchingImages: state.imagesReducer.fetchingUserImages } }
    function mapStateActionsToProps(dispatch) { return
    bindActionCreators(Actions, dispatch) }

    export default connect(mapStateToProps, mapStateActionsToProps)(MyImages);
```

The first thing this component does is make a call to the `fetchImages` action but, unlike the `<ImagesList />` component, it passes the username to only retrieve the pictures for the logged in user. When we create this action, we need to take this into account and receive an optional `userName` parameter to filter out the list of images we will retrieve.

Other than that, this component delegates most of its behavior to `<ImageGrid />` so that we can reuse the render capabilities for other users. Let's move on to `<ImageGrid />`.

ImageGrid

A simple scroll view and a list of images. This component is as simple as that, but it's configured in a way that allows the images to flow like a grid in an easy way:

```
/*** src/components/ImageGrid ***/

import React from 'react';
import {
    Image,
    TouchableOpacity,
    ScrollView,
    Dimensions,
    View,
    StyleSheet
} from 'react-native';

var {height, width} = Dimensions.get('window');

export default class ImagesGrid extends React.Component {
    render() {
        return (
            <ScrollView>
                <View style={styles.imageContainer}>
                    {
                        this.props.images &&
```

```
            this.props.images.map(img => {
              return (<Image style={styles.image}
              key={img.id} source={{uri: img.src}}/>);
            })
        }
      </View>
    </ScrollView>
  );
  }
}

const styles = StyleSheet.create({
  imageContainer: {
    flexDirection: 'row',
    alignItems: 'flex-start',
    flexWrap: 'wrap'
  },
  image: {
    width: (width/3 - 2),
    margin: 1,
    height: (width/3 - 2),
    resizeMode: 'cover'
  }
});
```

When styling the container, we use `flexWrap: 'wrap'` to ensure the images flow not only in the `row` direction but also spread to new lines when the device width is covered for a line of images. By setting `width` and `height` for each image to `width/3 - 2`, we ensure the container can fit three images per row, including two pixels for a small margin between them.

There are also several grid modules available through npm, but we have decided to build our own component for this matter, as we don't need extra functionality in the grid and we gain the flexibility to do it this way.

Those were all the screens and visual components we need in our image share app. Let's take a look now at the glue that makes them work together, the actions and the reducers.

Actions

As we see on our screens, there are only two actions needed for this app, fetchImages (for all users or for a specific user) and addImage:

```
/*** src/actions/index ***/

import api from '../api';

export function fetchImages(userId = null) {
  let actionName, actionNameSuccess, actionNameError;
  if(userId) {
    actionName = 'FETCH_USER_IMAGES';
    actionNameSuccess = 'FETCH_USER_IMAGES_SUCCESS';
    actionNameError = 'FETCH_USER_IMAGES_ERROR';
  } else {
    actionName = 'FETCH_IMAGES';
    actionNameSuccess = 'FETCH_IMAGES_SUCCESS';
    actionNameError = 'ADD_IMAGE_ERROR';
  }

  return dispatch => {
    dispatch({ type: actionName });
    api
      .fetchImages(userId)
      .then(images => {
        dispatch({
          type: actionNameSuccess,
          images
        })
      })
      .catch(error => {
        dispatch({
          type: actionNameError,
          error
        });
      });
  };
}

export function addImage(data = null) {
  return dispatch => {
    dispatch({ type: 'ADD_IMAGE' });
    api
      .addImage()
      .then(imageSrc => {
        dispatch({
```

```
            type: 'ADD_IMAGE_SUCCESS',
            imageSrc
          });
      })
      .catch(error => {
        dispatch({
          type: 'ADD_IMAGE_ERROR',
          error
        });
      });
    };
  }
```

Redux actions are just simple objects describing an event, including its payload. Since we are using `redux-thunk`, our *action creators* will return a function in which the Redux `dispatch` function will be called, passing the action. Let's take a closer look at our `addImage` action:

```
export function addImage(data = null) {
  return dispatch => {
    dispatch({ type: 'ADD_IMAGE' });
    api
      .addImage()
      .then(imageSrc => {
        dispatch({
          type: 'ADD_IMAGE_SUCCESS',
          imageSrc
        });
      })
      .catch(error => {
        dispatch({
          type: 'ADD_IMAGE_ERROR',
          error
        });
      });
    };
  }
```

The function we return starts by dispatching an action named ADD_IMAGE with no payload, as we just want to let Redux know that we are ready to make a network request to upload the image to our backend. Then, we make that request using our `api` (we will mock this call later). This request will return a promise, so we can attach `.then` and `.catch` callbacks to handle the response. If the response is positive (the image was properly uploaded), we will dispatch an ADD_IMAGE_SUCCESS action passing the URL for the uploaded image. If there is an error, we will dispatch an ADD_IMAGE_ERROR action covering all the possible states.

Most of the action creators work in a similar way when making network requests in *Redux* and *Thunk*. In fact, our action `fetchImages` is very similar to `addImage`, with one exception: it needs to check if `userId` was passed and issued a different set of actions instead, so the reducers can modify the state accordingly. Let's then take a look at the reducers, which will be handling all these actions.

Reducers

In Redux, reducers are functions in charge of updating the state as new actions happen. They receive the current state and the action (including any payload) and return a new `state` object. We won't go deep into how reducers work, we just need to understand their basic structure:

```
/*** src/reducers/index ***/

const initialState = {
  images: null,
  userImages: null,
  error: null,
  user: {
    id: 78261,
    name: 'Sharer1',
    pic: 'https://cdn.pixabay.com/photo/2015/07/20/12/53/
          man-852762_960_720.jpg'
  }
}

export default function (state = initialState, action) {
  switch(action.type){
    case 'FETCH_IMAGES':
      return Object.assign({}, state, {
        images: [],
        fetchingImages: true,
        error: null
      });
    case 'FETCH_IMAGES_SUCCESS':
      return Object.assign({}, state, {
        fetchingImages: false,
        images: action.images,
        error: null
      });
    case 'FETCH_IMAGES_ERROR':
      return Object.assign({}, state, {
        fetchingImages: false,
        images: null,
```

```
      error: action.error
    });
  case 'FETCH_USER_IMAGES':
    return Object.assign({}, state, {
      userImages: [],
      fetchingUserImages: true,
      error: null
    });
  case 'FETCH_USER_IMAGES_SUCCESS':
    return Object.assign({}, state, {
      fetchingUserImages: false,
      userImages: action.images,
      error: null
    });
  case 'FETCH_USER_IMAGES_ERROR':
    return Object.assign({}, state, {
      fetchingUserImages: false,
      userImages: null,
      error: action.error
    });
  case 'ADD_IMAGE':
    return Object.assign({}, state, {
      addingImage: true,
      error: null
    });
  case 'ADD_IMAGE_SUCCESS':
    let image = {
      id: Math.floor(Math.random() * 99999999),
      src: action.imageSrc,
      user: state.user
    }
    return Object.assign({}, state, {
      addingImage: false,
      images: [image].concat(state.images),
      userImages: [image].concat(state.images),
      error: null
    });
  case 'ADD_IMAGE_ERROR':
    return Object.assign({}, state, {
      addingImage: false,
      error: action.error
    });
  default:
    return state;
  }
}
```

Let's break this down:

```
const initialState = {
    images: null,
    userImages: null,
    error: null,
    user: {
        id: 78261,
        name: 'Sharer1',
        pic: 'https://cdn.pixabay.com/photo/2015/07/20/12/53/
            man-852762_960_720.jpg'
    }
}
```

We start with an initial state where all properties will be set to `null` except for `user`, which will contain mocked user data. This initial state is injected by default in the reducer on startup:

```
export default function (state = initialState, action) {

    ...

}
```

In the subsequent calls, Redux will inject the actual state after applying any actions. Inside this function, we have `switch` evaluating the type of each triggered action to modify the state according to that action and its payload. Let's take, for example, the `FETCH_IMAGES_SUCCESS` action:

```
case 'FETCH_IMAGES_SUCCESS':
    return Object.assign({}, state, {
        fetchingImages: false,
        images: action.images,
        error: null
    });
```

One of the rules in Redux is that reducers shouldn't mutate state, but return a new object after an action is triggered. Using `Object.assign`, we return a new object containing the current state plus the desired changes based on the action which just happened. In this case, we are setting the `fetchingImages` flag to `false` to let our components know that they can hide any activity indicator related to the action of fetching images. We also set the received list of images (from `actions.images`) in the key `images` of our state, so they can be injected into the components requiring them. Finally, we set the `error` flag to `null` to hide any errors we may have displayed because of a previous state.

As we mentioned before, every asynchronous action should be split into three separate actions to represent the three different states: asynchronous request pending, succeeded, and errored. This way, we will have three groups of actions for our app:

- FETCH_IMAGES, FETCH_IMAGES_SUCCESS, and FETCH_IMAGES_ERROR
- FETCH_USER_IMAGES, FETCH_USER_IMAGES_SUCCESS, and FETCH_USER_IMAGES_ERROR
- ADD_IMAGE, ADD_IMAGE_SUCCESS, and ADD_IMAGE_ERROR

It's important to note that we have separate cases for FETCH_IMAGES and FETCH_USER_IMAGES, as we want to keep two separate lists of images at the same time:

- A general one containing the images of all the people the user is following
- The list of the pictures the user has uploaded

The last missing piece is the API calls invoked from the action creators.

API

In a real-world app, we would place all the calls to our backend in a separate api folder. For educational purposes, we just mocked the two API calls that are core to our app, addImage and fetchImages:

```
/*** src/api/index ***/

export default {
  addImage: function(image) {
    return new Promise((resolve, reject) => {
      setTimeout(()=>{
        resolve( '<imgUrl>' );
      }, 3000)
    })
  },
  fetchImages: function(user = null){
    const images = [
      {id: 1, src: '<imgUrl>', user: {pic: '<imgUrl>', name: 'Naia'}},
      {id: 2, src: '<imgUrl>', user: {pic: '<imgUrl>',
       name: 'Mike_1982'}},
      {id: 5, src: '<imgUrl>', user: {pic: '<imgUrl>',
       name: 'Sharer1'}},
      {id: 3, src: '<imgUrl>', user: {pic: '<imgUrl>', name: 'Naia'}},
      {id: 6, src: '<imgUrl>', user: {pic: '<imgUrl>',
       name: 'Sharer1'}},
```

```
        {id: 4, src: '<imgUrl>', user: {pic: '<imgUrl>',
         name: 'Sharer1'}},
        {id: 7, src: '<imgUrl>', user: {pic: '<imgUrl>',
         name: 'Sharer1'}}

    ]
    return new Promise((resolve, reject) => {
      setTimeout(()=>{
        resolve( images.filter(img => !user || user === img.user.name)
      );
      }, 1500);
    })
  }
}
```

To simulate the network delay, we added some `setTimeouts` that will help in testing the activity indicators we set up to show the user network activity. We also used promises instead of plain callbacks to make our code easier to read. We also skipped the image URLs in these examples to make it more succinct.

Summary

We used Redux in this app, and that shaped the folder structure we use. Although using Redux requires some boilerplate code, it helps break up our codebase in a reasonable way and removes direct dependencies between containers or screens. Redux is definitely a great addition when we need to maintain a shared state between screens, so we will be using it further throughout the rest of this book. In more complex apps, we would need to build more reducers and possibly separate them by domain and use Redux `combineReducers`. Moreover, we would need to add more actions and create separate files for each group of actions. For example, we would need actions for login, logout, and register, which we could put together in a folder named `src/actions/user.js`. Then, we should move our image-related actions (currently in `index.js`) to `src/actions/images.js`, so we can modify `src/actions/index.js` to use it as a combinator for the user and images actions in case we want to have the ability to import all the actions in one go.

Redux also helps with testing as it isolates the app's business logic into the reducers, so we can focus on testing them thoroughly.

Mocking the API calls enables us to build a quick prototype for our app. When a backend is available, we can reuse those mockups for test purposes and replace `src/api/index.js` with real HTTP calls. In any case, it's a good idea to have a separate folder for all our API calls, so we can replace them easily if there are any backend changes.

You also learned how to build platform-specific code (Android-specific in our case), which is a very useful feature for most apps. Some companies prefer to write separate apps for each platform and only reuse their business logic code, which should be very easy in any Redux-based app as it resides in the reducers.

There is no specific API in React Native to control the device's camera, but we can use the `react-native-camera` module for it. This is an example of a library accessing iOS- and Android-native APIs to expose them in the React Native JavaScript world. In our next chapter, we will explore and cross that bridge between the native and the JavaScript world in React Native apps by building a guitar tuner app.

5
Guitar Tuner

React Native covers most of the components and APIs that are available in iOS and Android. Points such as UI components, navigation, or networking can be fully set up within our JavaScript code using React Native components, but not all the platform's capabilities have been mapped from the native world to the JavaScript world. Nonetheless, React Native offers a way to write real native code and have access to the full power of the platform. If React Native doesn't support a native feature that you need, you should be able to build it yourself.

In this chapter, we are going to use React Native's ability to enable our JavaScript code to communicate with custom native code; specifically, we will write a native module to detect frequencies coming from the device's microphone. These capabilities shouldn't be part of the day-to-day tasks for a React Native developer but, eventually, we may need to use modules or SDKs, which are only available on Objective-C, Swift, or Java.

For this chapter, we will focus on iOS, as we need to write native code which is outside the scope of this book. Porting this app to Android should be fairly simple as we can fully reuse the UI, but we will keep that out of this chapter to reduce the amount of native code written. Since we are focusing only on iOS, we will cover all the aspects of building the app, adding a splash screen and an icon, so it is ready to be submitted to the App Store.

 We will need a Mac and XCode to add and compile native code for this project.

Overview

The concept of how a guitar is tuned should be simple to understand: each of the six strings of a guitar emits a sound at a specific frequency when played open (that is when no fret is pushed). Tuning a guitar means tightening the string until a specific frequency is emitted. This is the list of frequencies each string should emit to be standard tuned:

String	Note	Frequency	Scientific pitch notation
1 (Highest)	e'	329.63 Hz	E4
2	b	246.94 Hz	B3
3	g	196.00 Hz	G3
4	d	146.83 Hz	D3
5	A	110.00 Hz	A2
6 (Lowest)	E	82.41 Hz	E2

The digital process of tuning a guitar will follow these steps:

1. Record a live sample of the frequencies captured through the device's microphone.
2. Find the most prominent frequency in that sample.
3. Calculate what is the closest frequency in the preceding table to detect what string is being played.
4. Calculate the difference between the frequency emitted and the standard tuned frequency for that string, so we can let the user correct the string tension.

There are also some pitfalls we need to overcome, like ignoring low volumes so that we don't confuse the user by detecting frequencies from sounds which are not coming from the strings.

For much of this process, we will use native code not only because we need to deal with features not available in React Native's API (for example, recording through the microphone), but also because we can perform complex calculations in a more effectual way. The algorithm we will be using here to detect the predominant frequency from the samples we take from the microphone is called the **Fast Fourier Transform** (**FFT**). We won't go into much detail here, but we will use a native library to perform these calculations.

The user interface for this app should be really simple as we only have one screen to show the user. The complexity will reside in the logic, rather than in displaying a beautiful interface, although we will use some images and animations to make it more appealing. It's important to keep in mind that the interface is what makes an app appealing in the App Store, so we won't neglect this aspect.

This is what our app will look like once it is finished:

At the top of the screen, our app displays an "analog" tuner displaying the frequency the guitar string is emitting. A red indicator will move inside the tuner to show if the guitar string is close to the tuned frequency. If the indicator is on the left side, it means the guitar string is at a lower frequency and needs to be tightened. Therefore, a user should try to make the indicator go to the middle of the tuner to ensure the string is tuned. This is a very intuitive way of showing how well a string is tuned.

However, we need to let the user know what string she is trying to tune. We can guess this by detecting what the closest tuned frequency is. Once we know what string was pushed, we will display it to the user in the bottom part of the screen where there is a representation of each of the strings plus the notes which should be played once the guitar is tuned. We will change the border color of the corresponding note to green to notify the user that the app detected a specific note.

Let's review the list of topics we will cover in this chapter:

- Running native code from JavaScript
- Animating images
- `<StatusBar />`
- `propTypes`
- Adding a splash screen
- Adding an icon

Setting up the folder structure

Let's initialize a React Native project using React Native's CLI. The project will be named `guitarTuner` and will be exclusively available for iOS:

```
react-native init --version="0.45.1" guitarTuner
```

As this is a single-screen app, we won't need a state management library such as Redux or MobX, so, we will use a simple folder structure:

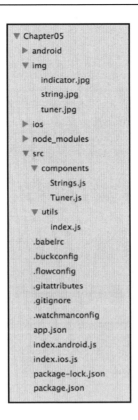

We have three images to support our custom interface:

- `indicator.jpg`: The red bar indicating how tuned a string is
- `tuner.jpg`: The background in which the indicator will move
- `string.jpg`: A representation of a guitar string

Our `src/` folder contains two subfolders:

- `components/`: This stores the `<Strings/>` component and the `<Tuner/>` component
- `utils/`: This holds a list of functions and constants which will be used in several parts of our app

Finally, the entry point of our app will be `index.ios.js`, as we will be building our app exclusively for the iOS platform.

Let's take a look at our `package.json` to identify what dependencies we will have:

```
/*** package.json ***/


{
        "name": "guitarTuner",
        "version": "0.0.1",
        "private": true,
        "scripts": {
                "start": "node node_modules/react-native/
                local-cli/cli.js start",
                "test": "jest"
        },
        "dependencies": {
                "react": "16.0.0-alpha.12",
                "react-native": "0.45.1"
        },
        "devDependencies": {
                "babel-jest": "20.0.3",
                "babel-preset-react-native": "2.0.0",
                "jest": "20.0.4",
                "react-test-renderer": "16.0.0-alpha.12"
        },
        "jest": {
                "preset": "react-native"
        }
}
```

As can be seen, there are no dependencies other than `react` and `react-native`, which are created by React Native's CLI when running the `init` script.

To obtain permission to record from the microphone, we also need to modify our `ios/guitarTuner/Info.plist` to add a *Microphone Usage Description*, which is a message to be displayed to the user to request access to the microphone on her device. We need to add these lines right before the last `</dict></plist>`:

```
<key>NSMicrophoneUsageDescription</key><key>NSMicrophoneUsageDescription</key>
<string>This app uses the microphone to detect what guitar
        string is being pressed.
</string>
```

With this last step, we should have the JavaScript part of our app ready to start coding. However, we still need to set up the native modules we will be using for recording and frequency detecting.

Writing the native module

We need XCode to write the native module, which will use the microphone to record samples and to analyze those samples to calculate the main frequency. As we are not interested in how these calculations are made, we will use an open source library to delegate most of the recording and FFT calculations. The library is named `SCListener` and a fork of it can be found at `https://github.com/emilioicai/sc_listener`.

We need to download the library and add its files to the project following these steps:

1. Navigate to the folder where our iOS project is: `<project_folder>/ios/`.
2. Double-click on `guitarTuner.xcodeproj`, which should open XCode.

3. Right-click on the `guitarTuner` folder and click on **Add Files to
"guitarTuner"...**:

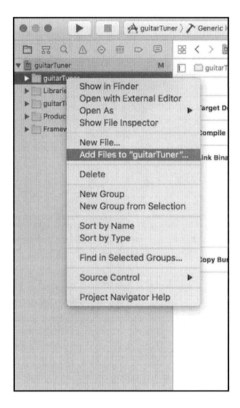

4. Select all the files from the downloaded `SCListener` library:

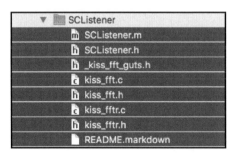

5. Click on **Accept**. You should end up with a file structure in XCode similar to this one:

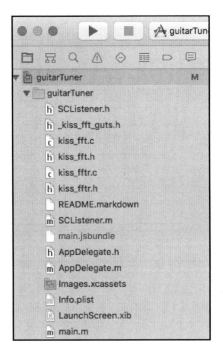

6. SCListener needs the AudioToolbox framework to be installed. Let's do this by clicking on the root of the project in XCode.

7. Select the **Build Phases** tab.

8. Go to **Link Binary with Libraries**.
9. Click on the + icon.
10. Select **AudioToolbox.framework**.

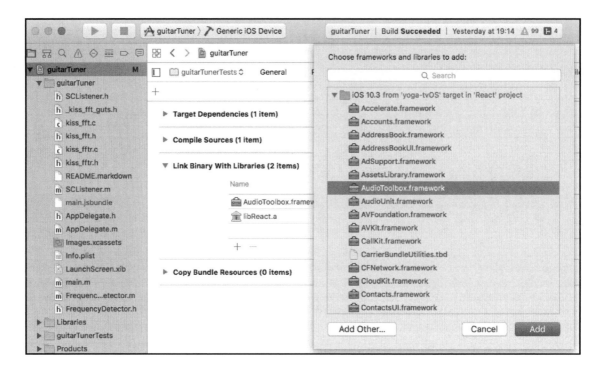

11. Now, let's add our module which will use `SCListener` and will send the data to React Native. Right-click on the `guitarTuner` folder and click on **New File**.

12. Add a header file named `FrequencyDetector.h`:

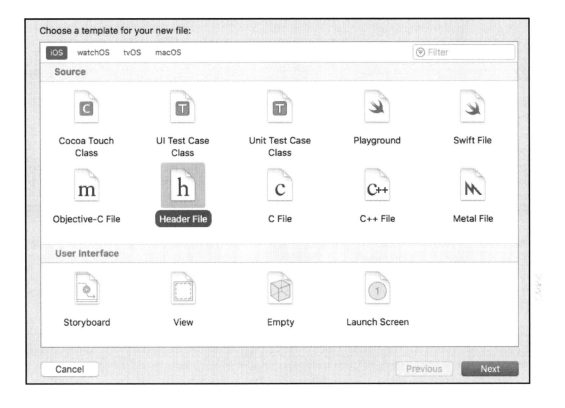

13. Let's repeat the process to add an implementation file for our module: right-click on the `guitarTuner` folder and click on **New File**.

14. Add an Objective-C file named `FrequencyDetector.m`:

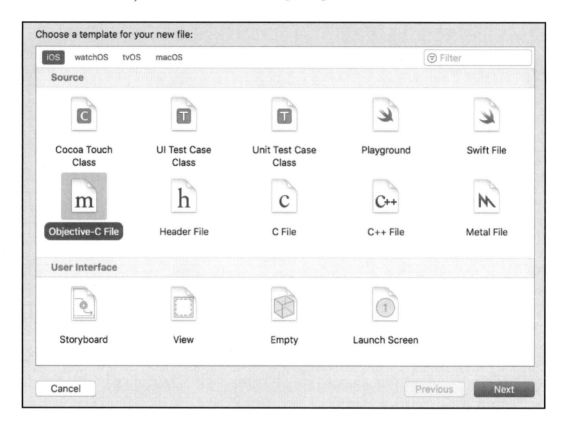

Our module `FrequencyDetector` is now ready to be implemented. Let's take a look at what `FrequencyDetector.h` should look like:

```
/*** FrequencyDetector.h ***/


#import <React/RCTBridgeModule.h>
#import <Accelerate/Accelerate.h>

@interface FrequencyDetector : NSObject
@end
```

It just imports two modules: `Accelerate` which is used to make the Fourier Transform calculations and `RCTBridgeModule`, which enables our native module to interact with our app's JavaScript code. Now, let's move to the implementation of the module:

```
/*** FrequencyDetector.m ***/


#import "FrequencyDetector.h"
#import "SCListener.h"

NSString *freq = @"";

@implementation FrequencyDetector

RCT_EXPORT_MODULE();


RCT_EXPORT_METHOD(getFrequency:(RCTResponseSenderBlock)callback)
{
  double power = [[SCListener sharedListener] averagePower];
  if(power < 0.03) { //ignore low volumes
    freq = @"0";
  } else {
    freq = [NSString stringWithFormat:@"%0.3f",
         [[SCListener sharedListener] frequency]];
  }
  callback(@[[NSNull null], freq]);
}

RCT_EXPORT_METHOD(initialise)
{
  [[SCListener sharedListener] listen];
}

@end
```

Even for non-Objective-C developers, this code should be easy to understand:

1. First, we import `SCListener`, the module which exposes methods to record from the device's microphone, and calculate the FFT from the recorded sample
2. Then, we expose two methods: `getFrequency` and `initialise`

The implementation of `getFrequency` is also quite simple. We only need to read the volume we detect on the microphone by calling `averagePower` on our SCListener shared instance. If the volume is strong enough, we decide a guitar string has been pushed so we update a variable named `freq`, which will be passed into a callback supplied from our JavaScript code. Note that sending data back to JavaScript can only be done through callbacks (or promises) due to the nature of the bridge between the native and the JavaScript code.

The way we expose methods from the native world into the JavaScript world is by using `RCT_EXPORT_METHOD`, a macro provided by `RCTBridgeModule`. We also need to let React Native know this module can be used from our JavaScript code. We do it by calling another macro: `RCT_EXPORT_MODULE`. That's all we need; from this moment on, we can access this module's methods with this:

```
import { NativeModules } from 'react-native';
var FrequencyDetector = NativeModules.FrequencyDetector;

FrequencyDetector.initialise();
FrequencyDetector.getFrequency((res, freq) => {});
```

As we can see, we pass a callback to `getFrequency` in which the current recorded frequency will be received. We can now use this value to calculate what string was pressed and how tuned it is. Let's take a look at how we are going to use this module in our app's JavaScript components.

index.ios.js

We already saw how we can access the method we exposed from the native module `FrequencyDetector`. Let's now see how we can use it within our components tree to update the state of our app:

```
/*** index.ios.js ***/

...

var FrequencyDetector = NativeModules.FrequencyDetector;

export default class guitarTuner extends Component {

  ...

  componentWillMount() {
    FrequencyDetector.initialise();
```

```
    setInterval(() => {
      FrequencyDetector.getFrequency((res, freq) => {
        let stringData = getClosestString(parseInt(freq));
        if(!stringData) {
          this.setState({
            delta: null,
            activeString: null
          });
        } else {
          this.setState({
            delta: stringData.delta,
            activeString: stringData.number
          });
        }
      });
    }, 500);
  }

  ...

});

AppRegistry.registerComponent('guitarTuner', () => guitarTuner);
```

Most of the logic will be placed in the `componentWillMount` method of our entry file. We need to initialize the `FrequencyDetector` module to start listening from the device's microphone and right after that, we call `setInterval` to repeatedly (every 0.5 seconds) invoke the `getFrequency` method of `FrequencyDetector` to get the updated prominent frequency. Every time we get a new frequency, we will check the guitar string which was most likely pressed by calling a support function named `getClosestString` and save the returned data in our component state. We will store this function in our `utils` file.

utils

Before continuing with `index.ios.js`, let's take a look at our `utils` file located in `src/utils/index.js`:

```
/*** src/utils/index.js ***/

const stringFrequencies = [
  { min: 287, max: 371, tuned: 329 },
  { min: 221, max: 287, tuned: 246 },
  { min: 171, max: 221, tuned: 196 },
  { min: 128, max: 171, tuned: 146 },
```

```
     { min: 96, max: 128, tuned: 110 },
     { min: 36, max: 96, tuned: 82}
];

export function getClosestString(freq) {
  let stringData = null;
  for(var i = 0; i < stringFrequencies.length; i++) {
    if(stringFrequencies[i].min < freq && stringFrequencies[i].max
       >= freq){
      let delta = freq - stringFrequencies[i].tuned; //absolute delta
      if(delta > 0){
        delta = Math.floor(delta * 100 / (stringFrequencies[i].max -
                           stringFrequencies[i].tuned));
      } else {
        delta = Math.floor(delta * 100 / (stringFrequencies[i].tuned -
                           stringFrequencies[i].min));
      }
      if(delta > 75) delta = 75; //limit deltas
      if(delta < -75) delta = -75;
      stringData = { number: 6 - i, delta } //relative delta
      break;
    }
  }
  return stringData;
}

export const colors = {
  black: '#1f2025',
  yellow: '#f3c556',
  green: '#3bd78b'
}
```

getClosestString is a function which, based on a provided frequency, will return a JavaScript object containing two values:

- number: This is the number from the guitar string which was most likely pressed
- delta: This is the difference between the frequency provided and the tuned frequency for the guitar string which was most likely pressed

We will also export a list of colors and their hex representation which will be used by some user interface components to keep consistency throughout the app.

After invoking `getClosestString`, we have enough information to build the state in our app. Of course, we need to provide this data to the tuner (to show how well-tuned the guitar string is) and to the string's representation (to show what guitar string was pressed). Let's take a look at the entire root component to see how this data is spread among components:

```
/*** index.ios.js ***/

import React, { Component } from 'react';
import {
  AppRegistry,
  StyleSheet,
  Image,
  View,
  NativeModules,
  Animated,
  Easing,
  StatusBar,
  Text
} from 'react-native';
import Tuner from './src/components/Tuner';
import Strings from './src/components/Strings';
import { getClosestString, colors } from './src/utils/';

var FrequencyDetector = NativeModules.FrequencyDetector;

export default class guitarTuner extends Component {
  state = {
    delta: null,
    activeString: null
  }

  componentWillMount() {
    FrequencyDetector.initialise();
    setInterval(() => {
      FrequencyDetector.getFrequency((res, freq) => {
        let stringData = getClosestString(parseInt(freq));
        if(!stringData) {
          this.setState({
            delta: null,
            activeString: null
          });
        } else {
          this.setState({
            delta: stringData.delta,
            activeString: stringData.number
          });
```

```
        }
      });
    }, 500);
  }

  render() {
    return (
      <View style={styles.container}>
        <StatusBar barStyle="light-content"/>
        <Tuner delta={this.state.delta} />
        <Strings activeString={this.state.activeString}/>
      </View>
    );
  }
}

const styles = StyleSheet.create({
  container: {
    backgroundColor: colors.black,
    flex: 1
  }
});

AppRegistry.registerComponent('guitarTuner', () => guitarTuner);
```

We will use two components to render the current pressed string (`<Strings/>`) and how tuned the pressed string is (`<Tuner/>`).

On top of that, we are using a React Native component named `<StatusBar/>`. `<StatusBar/>` allows the developer to choose the colors the app will show in the top bar where the carrier, time, battery level, and so on, are displayed:

As we want our app to have a black background, we decided to use a `light-content` bar style. This component allows us to hide the bar completely, change its background color (Android only), or hide network activity, among other options.

Let's move now to the components displaying all the visual components. We will start with `<Tuner/>`.

Tuner

Our `<Tuner/>` component comprises two elements: a background image dividing the screen into segments and an indicator which will move according to how well tuned the guitar string played is. To make it user-friendly, we will use animations to move the indicator, similar to the way analog tuners behave:

```
/*** src/components/Tuner/index ***/


import React, { Component } from 'react';
import {
  StyleSheet,
  Image,
  View,
  Animated,
  Easing,
  Dimensions
} from 'react-native';

import { colors } from '../utils/';

var {height, width} = Dimensions.get('window');

export default class Tuner extends Component {
  state = {
    xIndicator:  new Animated.Value(width/2)
  }

  static propTypes = {
    delta: React.PropTypes.number
  }

  componentWillReceiveProps(newProps) {
    if(this.props.delta !== newProps.delta) {
      Animated.timing(
        this.state.xIndicator,
        {
          toValue: (width/2) + (newProps.delta*width/2)/100,
          duration: 500,
          easing: Easing.elastic(2)
        }
      ).start();
    }
  }

  render() {
```

```
      let { xIndicator } = this.state;

      return (
        <View style={styles.tunerContainer}>
          <Image source={require('../../img/tuner.jpg')}
            style={styles.tuner}/>
          <Animated.Image source={require('../../img/indicator.jpg')}
            style={[styles.indicator, {left: xIndicator}]}/>
        </View>
      )
    }
  }

const styles = StyleSheet.create({
  tunerContainer: {
    flex: 1,
    backgroundColor: colors.black,
    marginTop: height * 0.05
  },
  tuner: {
    width,
    resizeMode: 'contain'
  },
  indicator: {
    position: 'absolute',
    top: 10
  }
});
```

We will use a component's `state` variable for the animation named `xIndicator`, which will store the value (in an animated way) of the position where the indicator should be. Remember, the closer to the center, the better tuned the string will be. We will update this value every time we receive a new `delta` prop from its parent using the `componentWillReceiveProps` method and the `Animated.timing` function to ensure the image is animated. To make it more realistic, we also added an easing function which will make the indicator bounce, a bit like a real analog indicator.

We also added a `propTypes` static attribute to our class for type checking. We will make sure this way our component receives a delta in the proper format.

Finally, remember how we exported a list of colors and their hex value in the `utils` file? We are using it here to show what color the background of this component will be.

Strings

The last component is a representation of the six strings of a guitar. When our `FrequencyDetector` native module detects which frequency is played, we will display which string has the ability to emit the closest frequency by changing the note's container border to green here:

Therefore, we need to accept one prop from its parent: the number of the active guitar string. Let's take a look at the code for this simple component:

```
/*** src/components/Strings ***/


import React, { Component } from 'react';
import {
  StyleSheet,
  Image,
  View,
  Text
} from 'react-native';

import { colors } from '../utils/';

const stringNotes = ['E','A','D','G','B','E'];

export default class Strings extends Component {
  static propTypes = {
    activeString: React.PropTypes.number
  }
```

```
render() {
  return (
    <View style={styles.stringsContainer}>
      {
        stringNotes.map((note, i) => {
          return (
            <View key={i} style={styles.stringContainer}>
              <Image source={require('../../img/string.jpg')}
                style={styles.string}/>
              <View style={[styles.noteContainer,
                {borderColor: (this.props.activeString === (i+1))
                  ? '#3bd78b' : '#f3c556'}]}>
                <Text style={styles.note}>
                  {note}
                </Text>
              </View>
            </View>
          )
        })
      }
    </View>
  );
}
}

const styles = StyleSheet.create({
  stringsContainer: {
    borderTopColor: colors.green,
    borderTopWidth: 5,
    justifyContent: 'space-around',
    flexDirection: 'row'
  },
  stringContainer: {
    alignItems: 'center'
  },
  note: {
    color: 'white',
    fontSize: 19,
    textAlign: 'center'
  },
  noteContainer: {
    top: 50,
    height: 50,
    width: 50,
    position: 'absolute',
    padding: 10,
    borderColor: colors.yellow,
    borderWidth: 3,
```

```
    borderRadius: 25,
    backgroundColor: colors.black
  }
});
```

We are rendering six images, one per guitar string, and justifying them using `space-around` to distribute them across the entire device screen, leaving two small spaces on both sides. We use a constant array containing the notes for each of the strings in a guitar to map them into the string representation. We will also use the prop `activeString` received from its parent to decide if we should show a yellow or a green border for each note.

We are again using `propTypes` to check the type of the provided prop (a number in this case).

This is all the code we need to build our guitar tuner. Let's add an icon and a splash screen now to make the app ready for submission to the App Store.

Adding an icon

Once we have our icon designed and saved as a large image, we need to resize it to all the formats Apple requires. In general, these are the sizes required:

- 20 x 20 px (iPhone Notification 2x)
- 60 x 60 px (iPhone Notification 3x)
- 58 x 58 px (iPhone Spotlight - iOS 5,6 2x)
- 67 x 67 px (iPhone Spotlight - iOS 5,6 3x)
- 80 x 80 px (iPhone Spotlight - iOS 7-10 2x)
- 120 x 120 px (iPhone Spotlight - iOS 7-10 3x && iPhone App ios 7-10 2x)
- 180 x 180 px (iPhone App ios 7-10 3x)

Since this is a very tedious process, we can use one of the online tools which automate all the resizing tasks by providing an image large enough. One of the most popular tools can be found at `https://resizeappicon.com/`.

Once we have our icon in the proper sizes, we need to add them to our XCode project. We will do this by clicking on `Images.xcassets` in XCode and adding each image with its corresponding size to each asset in this window:

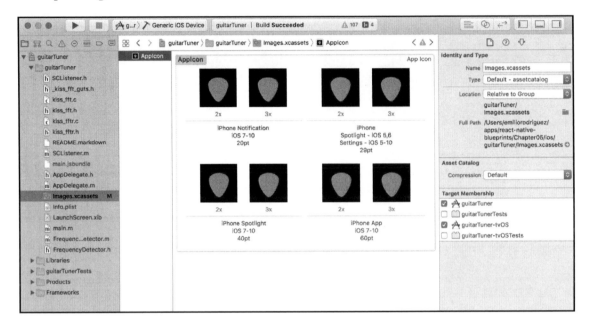

The next time we compile our app, we will see our new icon in the simulator (use *command + Shift + H* to show the home screen).

Adding a launch screen

The launch screen is an image iOS displays while your app is loading. There are several techniques to make this introduction pleasant for the user, like showing a preview of the user interface the user will see once the app is loaded. However, we will take a simpler approach: we will display the app logo with its title.

The easiest and more flexible way to do this is to use the interface builder in XCode by clicking on `LaunchScreen.xib`:

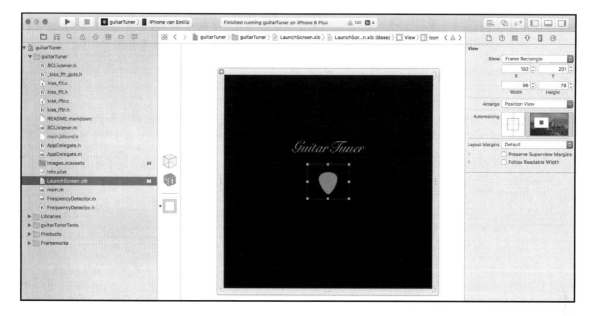

An interface builder is a WYSIWYG tool, which helps developers building responsive screens by dragging and dropping components into a container. We kept it simple and just added a label with the name of the app and the same logo we used on the app icon.

Another option could be to upload images as launch screens and remove the `LaunchScreen.xib` file, but then we would run the risk of stretching the images depending on which device the app is run, so the recommended approach is always to use the interface builder for launch screens.

Disabling the landscape mode

When testing our app, we need to test both landscape and portrait modes as both will be enabled by default. In the case of this app, we don't really need to have a landscape mode as it doesn't add any extra value to the portrait mode. Having decided this point, we need to disable the landscape mode to ensure we don't have any odd behavior in our user interface if the user orients the device as though for landscape mode. We will do this in XCode through the **General** tab when selecting the root of our project:

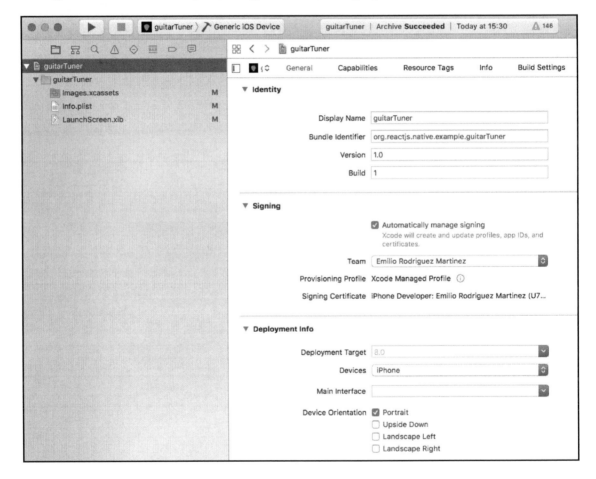

We need to uncheck both **Landscape Left** and **Landscape Right** options to allow only portrait mode in all cases.

Summary

The main challenge of this app was accessing a native module written in Objective-C from our JavaScript code. Fortunately, React Native has the means to ease the communication between those two worlds with relatively few lines of code.

We focused only on iOS for this app, but the reality is that building the same app in Android should follow a very similar process taking into account that we should build our native module in Java instead of Objective-C. Besides, we learned the process of including an icon and a launch screen in our app to complete the development cycle prior to release.

As we only had one screen in our app, we opted not to use any routing or state management libraries, which enabled us to keep the focus on the communication between our JavaScript code and the native module we implemented.

We also created some animations to emulate an analog tuner which gives an attractive and fun look to this app.

Besides the icon and the launch screen, we also took care of another visual element, which is important in many apps: the status bar. We saw how easy it is to change its content colors depending on what our app looks like. In this case, we opted for a dark background, so we needed light content in the status bar, although some apps (like games) may look better with no status bar at all.

We will move to a different kind of app in the next chapter: a messaging app.

6
Messaging App

One-to-one communication is the main use for mobile phones although, text messaging has been quickly replaced by direct messaging apps. In this chapter, we will build a messaging app in React Native with the support of Firebase, a mobile backend as a service that will free us from having to build a whole backend for our app. Instead, we will focus on handling the state of our app fully from the frontend. Of course, this may have security implications that need to be eventually tackled, but to keep the focus of this book on React Native's capabilities, we will stick with the approach of keeping all the logic inside our app.

Firebase is a real-time database built on self-synching collections of data, it plays very well with MobX, so we will use it again for controlling the state of our app. But in this chapter, we will dive deeper as we will build larger data stores, which will be injected in our component tree through the `mobx-react` connectors.

We will build the app to be used both with iOS and Android having some platform-specific code for navigation (we will use tabbed navigation for iOS and drawer navigation for Android).

To reduce the size of the code, in this chapter, we will set the focus on functionality rather than design. Most of the user interface will be plain and simple, but trying to keep usability in mind. Moreover, we will use a `react-native-gifted` chat for our chat screen--a pre-built React Native component to render chat rooms based on a list of messages.

Overview

A messaging app requires more work than the apps we reviewed in previous chapters, as it needs a user management system comprising of logging in, registering, and logging out. We will reduce the complexity of building this system using Firebase as a backend. Together with its user management system, we will use their push notifications system to notify users when new messages are sent to them. Firebase also gives an analytics platform, a lambda functions service, and a storage system for free, but the feature we will take the most profit from is their real-time database. We will store our user's profile, messages, and chats data there.

Let's take a look at what our app will look like to have a mental image of the screens we will be building:

First screen will be a login/registration screen because we need our users to provide a name and some credentials to attach their device to a specific account, so they can receive push notifications for each message they need to receive. Both authentication methods are validated using Firebase's API and would result in the chats screen when they are successful:

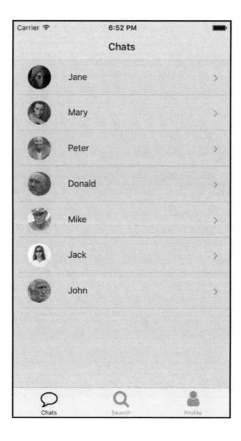

When pressing a contact in the contacts list, the app will display the conversation with the selected contact in the chat screen:

The chats screen will show up all the chats that were started for the logged in user. Initially, this screen will be empty as the user won't have initiated any chats. To start a conversation, the user should go to the search screen in order to find some contacts:

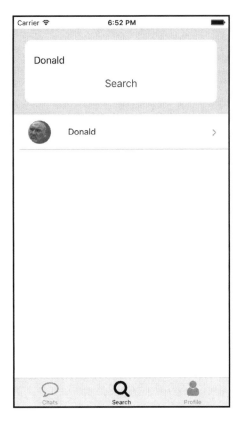

This is a simple screen where the user can enter the contact name to search for it in the database. If there is a match on the name of the contact; the user will be able to tap on it to get the conversation started. From that point on, the conversation will show in the chat screen.

The last screen is the profile screen:

This screen is just a mean to log the current user out. When extending the app, we could add more features such as changing the avatar or the username.

While the app will look very similar on Android, navigation will be replaced by a drawer from which all the screens will be available. Let's take a look at the Android version:

The login/registration screen has standard text input and button components for Android:

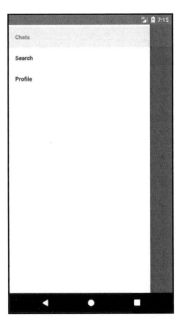

Once the user logs in, he/she can navigate through all the screens by opening the drawer through the sliding finger gesture. The screen that opens by default after login is the chats screens where we will list the list of open conversations the user has:

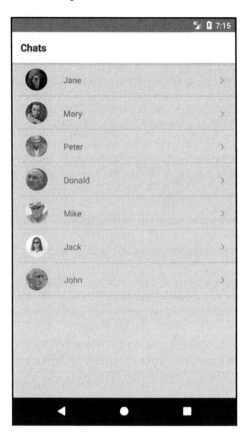

From this screen, the user can press a specific conversation to list the messages on it:

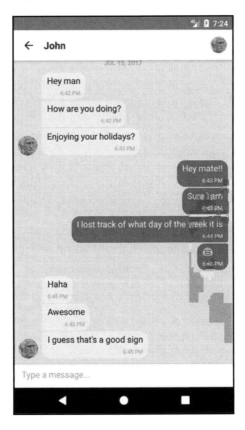

The next screen is the search screen, which will be used to search for other users and start conversations with them:

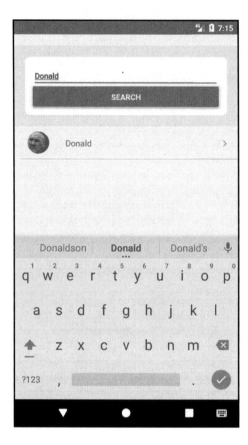

The last screen is the profile screen where the **LOGOUT** button can be found:

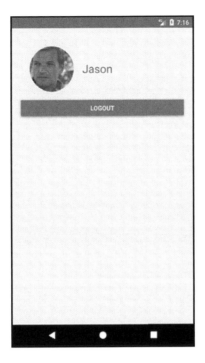

The app will work on both platforms in portrait and landscape mode out of the box:

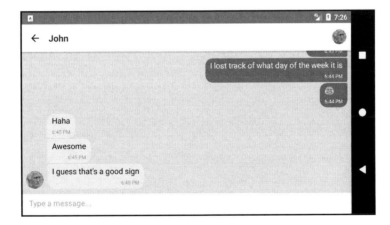

As we can imagine, this app will require of a powerful backend environment to store our users, messages, and statuses. Moreover, we will require a Push Notifications platform to notify users when they receive any messages. Since we are focusing in React Native in this book, we will delegate all this backend work to one of the most popular Mobile Backend as a Services (MBaaS) in the mobile world: Firebase

Before start coding, we will spend some time setting up our Firebase's push notifications service and real-time database to better understand what kind of data we will be dealing with in our app.

In summary, we will go through the following topics in this chapter:

- Complex Redux in React Native
- Firebase real-time database
- Firebase push notifications
- Firebase user management
- Forms

Let's start by reviewing the data models we will be using and how our app will connect with Firebase for syncing its data.

Firebase

Firebase is a **Mobile Backend as a Service** (**MBaaS**), which means that it provides mobile developers with all the backend necessities, such as user management, no SQL database, and a push notification server. It integrates easily with React Native through an official node package, which brings the database connection for free. Unfortunately, Firebase doesn't offer a JavaScript SDK for their push notifications service, but there are several React Native libraries filling that gap by bridging Firebase's iOS and Java SDKs with a JavaScript interface. We will be using `react-native-fcm` as it is the most mature in its field.

Before building an app on top of a Firebase MBaaS, you need to create a project for it. This is a free process that is explained in Firebase's website `https://firebase.google.com/`. Although this process is not directly related to React Native, it's a good starting point to understand how to set up and use a MBaaS for our apps. Most of the configuring can be finished in a matter of minutes just by following the tutorials available on Firebase's documentation site. The benefits of setting up this MBaaS make those minutes worth the time and initial hassle.

To set up Firebase and connect our app to the correct project, we need to use the `configuration for the web` snippet we can find in the **Settings** screen inside our Firebase project's dashboard. We added this initialization snippet on `src/firebase.js`:

```
import firebase from 'firebase';

var firebaseConfig = {
  apiKey: "<Your Firebase API key>",
  authDomain: "<Your Firebase Auth domain>",
  databaseURL: "<Your Firebase database URL>",
  projectId: "<Your Firebase projectId>",
  storageBucket: "<Your Firebase storageBucket>",
  messagingSenderId: "<Your messaging SenderId>"
};

export const firebaseApp = firebase.initializeApp(firebaseConfig);
```

Once the project is set up, we can start taking a look at how our database is going to be structured.

Real-time database

Firebase allows mobile developers to store and sync data between users and devices in real time using a cloud-hosted, noSQL database. Updated data syncs across connected devices in milliseconds and data remains available if your app goes offline, providing a great user experience regardless of network connectivity.

Three data models come into the picture when thinking about the basic data a one-to-one communication app should handle:

- `users`: This will store avatars, names, and push notification tokens. There is no need to store authentication data here as it is handled through a different Firebase API (authentication API).
- `messages`: We will save each message on each chat room separately for easy retrieval using the chat room ID as a key.
- `chats`: All the information about the opened chats will be stored here.

To understand how we will request and use the data in our app, let's see a gist of the example data we can actually use for testing:

```json
{
  "chats" : {
    "--userId1--" : {
      "--userId2----userId1--" : {
        "contactId" : "--userId2--",
        "image" : "https://images.com/person2.jpg",
        "name" : "Jason"
      }
    },
    "--userId2--" : {
      "--userId2----userId1--" : {
        "contactId" : "--userId1--",
        "image" : "https://images.com/person1.jpg",
        "name" : "John"
      }
    }
  },
  "messages" : {
    "--userId2----userId1--" : {
      "-KpEwU8sr01vHSy3qvRY" : {
        "_id" : "2367ad00-301d-46b5-a7b5-97cb88781489",
        "createdAt" : 1500284842672,
        "text" : "Hey man!",
        "user" : {
          "_id" : "--userId2--",
          "name" : "Jason"
        }
      }
    }
  },
  "users" : {
    "--userId1--" : {
      "name" : "John",
      "notificationsToken" : ""
    },
    "--userId2--" : {
      "name" : "Jason",
      "notificationsToken" : "--notificationsId1--"
    }
  }
}
```

We organized our data in a way it will be easy for the messaging app to retrieve and synchronize. Instead of normalizing the data structure, we introduced some data duplication to increase speed during data retrieval and simplify the frontend code to the maximum.

The `users` collection holds the users' data using the user ID as a key (`--user1--`, and `--user2--`). These user IDs are retrieved automatically by Firebase during registration/login. Each user has a notification token, which is an identifier for the device the user is logged in with the push notifications service. When the user logs out, the notifications token is removed, so messages sent to this user will be stored, but not notified to any device.

The `chats` collection stores each user's chat list by user ID. Each chat has its own ID (a concatenation of both user IDs) and will be duplicated as every user on that chat should have a copy of the chat data. In each copy, there is enough information for the other user to build up their chat screen.

The `messages` collection is stored in a separate collection, which can be referenced by that ID. Each chat ID points to a list of messages (only one in this example) where all the data needed by the chat screen is stored. There is also some duplication in this collection as some user data is stored together with each message to reduce the number of requests needed when building a chat screen.

A full tutorial on how to read and write data in Firebase's real-time database can be found on their website (`https://firebase.google.com/docs/database/`), but we will take a quick look at the methods we will be using in this chapter.

Reading data from Firebase's database

There are two ways for retrieving data from Firebase's database. The first one sets a listener that will be called every time the data changes, so we only need to set it up once for the entire lifetime of our app:

```
firebaseApp.database().ref('/users/' + userId).on('value', (snapshot) => {
  const userObj = snapshot.val();
  this.name = userObj.name;
  this.avatar = userObj.avatar;
});
```

As we can see, in order to retrieve a snapshot of data, we need to call the `database()` method in our `firebaseApp` object (the one we created in our `src/firebase.js` file). Then, we will have a `database` object where we can call the `ref('<uri>')` on it passing the URI, where the data is stored. That will return a reference to the piece of data pointed by that URI. We can go for the `on('value', callback)` method, which will attach a callback passing the snapshot of data. Firebase always returns objects as snapshots, so we need to transform them into plain data ourselves. In this example, we want to retrieve an object with two keys (`name` and `avatar`), so we only need to call the `val()` method on the snapshot to retrieve a plain object containing the data.

If we don't need the retrieved data to be automatically synched every time it is updated, we could have used the `once()` method instead of `on()`:

```
import firebase from 'firebase';
import { firebaseApp } from '../firebase';

firebaseApp.database().ref('/users/' + userId).once('value')
.then((snapshot) => {
  const userObj = snapshot.val();
  this.name = userObj.name;
  this.avatar = userObj.avatar;
});
```

The callback receiving snapshot will only be called once.

Updating data in Firebase's database

Writing data in a Firebase database can also be done in two different ways:

```
firebaseApp.database().ref('/users/' + userId).update({
  name: userName
});
```

`update()` changes the object referenced by the supplied URI according to the keys and values passed as a parameter. The rest of the object is left intact.

On the other hand, `set()` will replace the object in the database with the one we provide as a parameter:

```
firebaseApp.database().ref('/users/' + userId).set({
  name: userName,
  avatar: avatarURL
});
```

Finally, if we want to add a new snapshot of data but we want Firebase to generate an ID for it, we can use the push method:

```
firebaseApp.database().ref('/messages/' + chatId).push().set(message);
```

Authentication

We will use Firebase authentication services, so we don't need to worry about storing login credentials, handling forgotten passwords, or verifying emails on our side. These and other related tasks come for free with Firebase authentication services.

In order to activate login and registration through email and password, we need to enable this method as a session sign-in method in our Firebase dashboard. More information about how to do this can be found on Firebase's website at https://firebase.google.com/docs/auth/web/password-auth.

In our app, we only need to use the provided Firebase SDK for login:

```
firebase.auth().signInWithEmailAndPassword(username, password)
    .then(() => {
        //user is logged in
    })
    .catch(() => {
        //error logging in
    })
})
```

For registration, we can use the following code:

```
firebase.auth().createUserWithEmailAndPassword(email, password)
.then((user) => {
    //user is registered
})
.catch((error) => {
    //error registering
})
```

All the token handling will be taken care of by Firebase, and we only need to add a listener to make sure our app is updated when the authentication status changes:

```
firebase.auth().onAuthStateChanged((user) => {
    //user has logged in or out
}
```

Setting up the folder structure

Let's initialize a React Native project using React Native's CLI. The project will be named `messagingApp` and will be available for iOS and Android devices:

```
react-native init --version="0.45.1" messagingApp
```

We will be using MobX to manage state in our app, so we will need a folder for our stores. The rest of the folder structure is standard to most React apps:

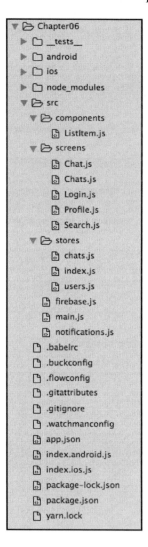

We need five screens (Chats, Chat, Login, Profile, and Search), a component (ListItem) and two stores (chats and users), which will be available through the stores/index.js file. There are also two helpers that we will be using to support our app:

- notifications.js: All the logic related to push notifications will be stored in this file
- firebase.js: This includes the configuration and initialization of Firebase SDK

Since we will be using MobX and several other dependencies, let's take a look at our package.json file to understand what packages we will be using:

```
/*** package.json ***/

{
        "name": "messagingApp",
        "version": "0.0.1",
        "private": true,
        "scripts": {
                "start": "node node_modules/react-native/local-cli
                        /cli.js start",
                "test": "jest"
        },
        "dependencies": {
                "firebase": "^4.1.3",
                "mobx": "^3.2.0",
                "mobx-react": "^4.2.2",
                "react": "16.0.0-alpha.12",
                "react-native": "0.45.1",
                "react-native-fcm": "^7.1.0",
                "react-native-gifted-chat": "^0.2.0",
                "react-native-keyboard-aware-scroll-view": "^0.2.9",
                "react-native-vector-icons": "^4.2.0",
                "react-navigation": "^1.0.0-beta.11"
        },
        "devDependencies": {
                "babel-jest": "20.0.3",
                "babel-plugin-transform-decorators-legacy": "^1.3.4",
                "babel-preset-react-native": "2.1.0",
                "jest": "20.0.4",
                "react-test-renderer": "16.0.0-alpha.12"
        },
        "jest": {
                "preset": "react-native"
        }
}
```

Some of the npm packages we will be using are:

- `firebase`: Firebase's SDK for authentication and database connection
- `mobx`: MobX will handle our app state
- `react-native-fcm`: Firebase's SDK for push messaging
- `react-native-gifted-chat`: A library for rendering chat rooms including date separation, avatars, and many other features
- `react-native-keyboard-aware-scroll-view`: A library that ensures the on-screen keyboard doesn't hide any focused text input when working with forms
- `react-native-vector-icons`: We will use Font Awesome icons for this app
- `react-navigation`: We will have a drawer, a tabbed, and a stack navigator handling the screens in our app
- `babel-plugin-transform-decorators-legacy`: This library allows us to use decorators (with the legacy @ syntax) which is quite useful when working with MobX

After running `npm install`, we will have our app ready to start coding. As it happened in previous apps, the entry point for our messaging app will be the same code both in `index.ios.js` for iOS and in `index.android.js` for Android:

```
/*** index.ios.js and index.android.js ***/

import React from 'react'
import { AppRegistry } from 'react-native';
import App from './src/main';

import { Provider } from 'mobx-react/native';
import { chats, users } from './src/stores';

class MessagingApp extends React.Component {
  render() {
    return (
      <Provider users={users} chats={chats}>
        <App/>
      </Provider>
    )
  }
}

AppRegistry.registerComponent('messagingApp', () => MessagingApp);
```

This is a standard way to start up a React Native app working with MobX--a `<Provider />` is supplied as the root element to inject the two stores (`users` and `chats`) into the screens in our app. All the initializing and navigation logic has been deferred to the `src/main.js` file:

```
/*** src/main.js ***/

import React from 'react'
import { DrawerNavigator, TabNavigator } from 'react-navigation'
import { Platform, View } from 'react-native'
import { observer, inject } from 'mobx-react/native'

import Login from './screens/Login'
import Chats from './screens/Chats'
import Profile from './screens/Profile'
import Search from './screens/Search'
import { users, chats } from './stores'

let Navigator;
if(Platform.OS === 'ios'){
  Navigator = TabNavigator({
    Chats: { screen: Chats },
    Search: { screen: Search },
    Profile: { screen: Profile }
  }, {
    tabBarOptions: {
      inactiveTintColor: '#aaa',
      activeTintColor: '#000',
      showLabel: true
    }
  });
} else {
  Navigator = DrawerNavigator({
    Chats: { screen: Chats },
    Search: { screen: Search },
    Profile: { screen: Profile }
  });
}

@inject('users') @observer
export default class App extends React.Component {
  constructor() {
    super();
  }

  render() {
    if(this.props.users.isLoggedIn){
```

```
        return <Navigator/>
    } else {
        return <Login/>
    }
  }
}
```

The first thing we can see on the `src/main.js` file is that we will use different navigators, depending on which platform we are running the app: iOS will open a tabbed navigator, while Android will open a drawer-based navigator.

Then, we see a line we will be repeating in many components in our app:

```
@inject('users') @observer
```

This is the way to tell MobX this component needs to receive the `users` store. MobX will then pass it as a prop to this component and therefore we can use all the methods and attributes it holds. In this case, we are interested in the `isLoggedIn` attribute to present the user with the `<Login />` screen if they are still not logged in. Since MobX will inject this attribute as a property in our component, the right way to access it will be `this.props.users.isLoggedIn`.

Before continuing building components, let's take a look at the stores we will be using throughout this chapter to better understand what data and actions are available.

Users store

This store is responsible for holding all the data and logic surrounding users, but also helps the `chats` store initializing when a user is logged in:

```
/*** src/stores/users.js ***/

import {observable, computed, map, toJS, action} from 'mobx';
import chats from './chats'
import firebase from 'firebase';
import { firebaseApp } from '../firebase';
import notifications from '../notifications'

class Users {
        @observable id = null;
        @observable isLoggedIn = false;
        @observable name = null;
        @observable avatar = null;
        @observable notificationsToken = null;
```

```
@observable loggingIn = false;
@observable registering = false;
@observable loggingError = null;
@observable registeringError = null;

@action login = function(username, password) {
        //login with Firebase email/password method
}

@action logout = function() {
        //logout from Firebase authentication service
}

@action register = function(email, password, name) {
        //register through firebase authentication service
}

@action setNotificationsToken(token) {
        //store the notifications token for this device
}

searchUsers(name) {
        //helper for searching users by name in the database
}

constructor() {
        this.bindToFirebase();
}

bindToFirebase() {
        //Initialise connection to Firebase user
        //authentication status and data
}
}

const users = new Users();

export default users;
```

These are all the attributes and methods we need for this store. There are several flags (those attributes containing a verb in its -ing form) to note network activity. Let's implement each method now:

```
@action login = function(username, password) {
        this.loggingIn = true;
        this.loggingError = null;
        firebase.auth().signInWithEmailAndPassword(username, password)
        .then(() => {
```

```
            this.loggingIn = false;
            notifications.init((notificationsToken) => {
                    this.setNotificationsToken(notificationsToken);
            });
    })
    .catch((error) => {
            this.loggingIn = false;
            this.loggingError = error.message;
    });
}
```

Logging in with Firebase is as simple as calling `signInWithEmailAndPassword` on their authentication SDK. If the login is successful, we will initialize the notifications module to enable the device to receive push notifications. We will follow the opposite path on logout:

```
@action logout = function() {
        notifications.unbind();
        this.setNotificationsToken('');
        firebase.auth().signOut();
}
```

In the registration action, besides setting the appropriate flags for network activity, we need to validate the user entered a name, initialize the notifications, and store the name in the database:

```
@action register = function(email, password, name) {
        if(!name || name == '') {
                this.registering = false;
                this.registeringError = 'Name was not entered';
                return;
        }
        this.registering = true;
        this.registeringError = null;
        firebase.auth().createUserWithEmailAndPassword(email, password)
        .then((user) => {
                this.registering = false;
                notifications.init((notificationsToken) => {
                        this.setNotificationsToken(notificationsToken);
                });
                firebaseApp.database().ref('/users/' + user.uid).set({
                        name: name
                });
        })
        .catch((error) => {
                this.registering = false;
                this.registeringError = error.message;
        })
}
```

Setting the notification token is just a simple update in the database:

```
@action setNotificationsToken(token) {
        if(!this.id) return;
        this.notificationsToken = token;
        firebaseApp.database().ref('/users/' + this.id).update({
                notificationsToken: token
        });
}
```

searchUsers() is not marked as @action, as it won't modify the state of our app, but only search and return a list of users with the provided name in the database:

```
searchUsers(name) {
        return new Promise(function(resolve) {
                firebaseApp.database().ref('/users/').once('value')
                .then(function(snapshot) {
                        let foundUsers = [];
                        const users = snapshot.val();
                        for(var id in users) {
                                if(users[id].name === name) {
                                        foundUsers.push({
                                                name: users[id].name,
                                                avatar:
                                                users[id].avatar,
                                                notificationsToken:
                                                users[id].
                                                notificationsToken,
                                                id
                                        });
                                }
                        }
                        resolve(foundUsers);
                });
        });
}
```

We will return the result as a promise, due to the asynchronous nature of the request we are making.

Finally, `bindToFirebase()` will attach the attributes in this store to data snapshots in Firebase's database. This method is called by the constructor, so it serves as initialization for the user data. It's important to note that this data will be updated when the authentication status changed to always reflect the most up to date data for the user:

```
bindToFirebase() {
  return firebase.auth().onAuthStateChanged((user) => {
    if(this.chatsBind && typeof this.chatsBind.off === 'function')
      this.chatsBind.off();
    if(this.userBind && typeof this.userBind.off === 'function')
      this.userBind.off();

    if (user) {
      this.id = user.uid;
      this.isLoggedIn = true;
      this.chatsBind = chats.bindToFirebase(user.uid);
      this.userBind = firebaseApp.database().ref('/users/' + this.id).
                                      on('value', (snapshot) =>
    {
        const userObj = snapshot.val();
        if(!userObj) return;
        this.name = userObj.name;
        this.avatar = userObj.avatar;
      });
    } else {
      this.id = null;
      this.isLoggedIn = false;
      this.userBind = null;
      this.name = null;
      this.avatar = null;
    }
  });
}
```

We will store the listeners for the chat data (as `this.chatsBind`) and for the user data (as `this.userBind`), so we can remove them (by calling the `off()` method) before attaching new listeners on every `auth` state change.

Chats store

This store is responsible for holding all the data and logic surrounding chats and messages, but it also helps the `chats` store initializing when a user is logged in:

```
/*** src/stores/chats.js ***/

import { observable, computed, map, toJS, action } from 'mobx';
import { AsyncStorage } from 'react-native'

import { firebaseApp } from '../firebase'
import notifications from '../notifications'

class Chats {
  @observable list;
  @observable selectedChatMessages;
  @observable downloadingChats = false;
  @observable downloadingChat = false;

  @action addMessages = function(chatId, contactId, messages) {
    //add a list of messages to a chat
  }

  @action selectChat = function(id) {
    //set a chat as selected and retrieve all the messages for it
  }

  @action add(user1, user2) {
    //add a new chat to the list of chats for the users in it
  }

  bindToFirebase(userId) {
    //listen for the list of chats in Firebase to update the
    @observable list
  }
}

const chats = new Chats()
export default chats;
```

We will store the list of open chats the user has in `@observable list`. When a user selects one chat, we will download and synchronize the list of messages on that chat to `@observable selectedChatMessages`. Then, we will have a couple of flags to let the user know when we are downloading data from the Firebase database.

Let's take a look at each method individually. We will start with `addMessages`:

```
@action addMessages = function(chatId, contactId, messages) {
  if(!messages || messages.length < 1) return;

  messages.forEach((message) => {
    let formattedMessage = {
      _id: message._id,
      user: {
        _id: message.user._id,
      }
    };
    if(message.text) formattedMessage.text = message.text;
    if(message.createdAt) formattedMessage.createdAt =
      message.createdAt/1;
    if(message.user.name) formattedMessage.user.name =
      message.user.name;
    if(message.user.avatar) formattedMessage.user.avatar =
      message.user.avatar;
    if(message.image) formattedMessage.image = message.image;

    //add the message to the chat
    firebaseApp.database().ref('/messages/' +
      chatId).push().set(formattedMessage);

    //notify person on the chat room
    firebaseApp.database().ref('/users/' + contactId).once('value')
    .then(function(snapshot) {
      var notificationsToken = snapshot.val().notificationsToken;
      notifications.sendNotification(notificationsToken, {
        sender: message.user.name,
        text: message.text,
        image: message.user.image,
        chatId
      });
    });
  });
}
```

This method receives three parameters:

- `chatId`: The ID for the chat in which the messages will be added.
- `contactId`: The ID for the user to whom we are sending the message. This will be used to send a notification to the user's contact.
- `messages`: This is an array with all the messages we want to add to the chat.

We will loop through the list of messages, formatting the message the way we want to store it. Then, we will call the `set()` method on a database reference to save the new message in Firebase's database. Finally, we need to send the notification to our contact, so we retrieve their notifications token by querying the `users` collection by their `contactId`.

Sending notifications is normally handled by the backend, but since we are setting all the logic on the app itself, we need to build a function to send notifications. We have done this in our notifications
module: `notifications.sendNotification(notificationsToken, data);`.

Let's see what happens when we select a chat to display the messages for it:

```
@action selectChat = function(id) {
  this.downloadingChat = true;
  if(this.chatBind && typeof this.chatBind.off === 'function')
  this.chatBind.off();
  this.chatBind = firebaseApp.database().ref('/messages/' + id)
  .on('value', (snapshot) => {
    this.selectedChatMessages = [];
    this.downloadingChat = false;
    const messagesObj = snapshot.val();
    for(var id in messagesObj) {
      this.selectedChatMessages.push({
        _id: id,
        text: messagesObj[id].text,
        createdAt: messagesObj[id].createdAt,
        user: {
          _id: messagesObj[id].user._id,
          name: messagesObj[id].user.name,
          avatar: messagesObj[id].user.avatar
        },
        image: messagesObj[id].image
      });
    }
  });
}
```

The main piece of functionality here is attaching a listener to the messages/chat ID collection, which will sync the `this.selectedChatMessages` observable with the list of messages for the selected chat in the database. This means that every time a new message is stored in Firebase, `this.selectedChatMessages` will be synced to reflect it. This is how the `on()` method in the Firebase SDK works: we pass a callback, which we can use to synchronize the real-time database with our app's state.

Adding a new chat will be done using the `add()` method:

```
@action add(user1, user2) {
  return new Promise(function(resolve, reject) {
    firebaseApp.database().ref('/chats/' + user1.id + '/' + user1.id +
    user2.id).set({
      name: user2.name,
      image: user2.avatar,
      contactId: user2.id
    }).then(() => {
      firebaseApp.database().ref('/chats/' + user2.id + '/'
                                    + user1.id +
      user2.id).set({
        name: user1.name,
        image: user1.avatar,
        contactId: user1.id
      }).then(() => {
        resolve();
      })
    })
  });
}
```

Here, we are building and returning a promise that will be resolved when the two chats (one per each user participating in the chat) are updated. These two database updates can be seen as the duplication of data, but it will also reduce the data structure complexity and therefore our code base readability.

The last method in this store is `bindToFirebase()`:

```
bindToFirebase(userId) {
  this.downloadingChats = true;
  return firebaseApp.database().ref('/chats/' + userId).
                            on('value', (snapshot) => {
    this.downloadingChats = false;
    const chatsObj = snapshot.val();
    this.list = [];
    for(var id in chatsObj) {
      this.list.push({
        id,
        name: chatsObj[id].name,
        image: chatsObj[id].image,
        contactId: chatsObj[id].contactId
      });
    }
  });
}
```

As we saw in our `users` store, this method will be called when the user logs in and attaches a listener to the `chats/<userId>` snapshot of data to keep all the chats data synched with the database on the `this.list` attribute.

As a convenience, we will group both stores in `src/stores/index.js`, so we can import them both on one line of code:

```
/*** src/stores/index.js ***/

import users from './users';
import chats from './chats';

export {
  users,
  chats
};
```

This is all about the stores we will be using. As we can see, most of the business logic is handled here so it can be thoroughly tested. Let's move now to the helper we will use for notifications.

Push notifications using Firebase

Firebase incorporates a push notification service for iOS and Android, but it unfortunately doesn't provide any JavaScript on their SDK to use it. For this matter, an open source library was created bridging the Objective-C and Java SDKs into a React Native module: `react-native-fcm`.

We won't cover the installation of this module in this book, as it's a changing process that can be better followed on its repository at `https://github.com/evollu/react-native-fcm`.

We decided to abstract the logic for this module on our `src/notifications.js` file to make it available for every component while keeping its maintainability. Let's take a look at this file:

```
/*** src/notifications.js ***/

import {Platform} from 'react-native';
import FCM, {FCMEvent, RemoteNotificationResult,
WillPresentNotificationResult, NotificationType} from 'react-native-fcm';

let notificationListener = null;
let refreshTokenListener = null;
const API_URL = 'https://fcm.googleapis.com/fcm/send';
```

```
const FirebaseServerKey = '<Your Firebase Server Key>';

const init = (cb) => {
  FCM.requestPermissions();
  FCM.getFCMToken().then(token => {
    cb(token)
  });
  refreshTokenListener = FCM.on(FCMEvent.RefreshToken, (token) => {
    cb(token);
  });
}

const onNotification = (cb) => {
  notificationListener = FCM.on(FCMEvent.Notification, (notif) => {
    cb(notif);

    if(Platform.OS ==='ios'){
      switch(notif._notificationType){
        case NotificationType.Remote:
          notif.finish(RemoteNotificationResult.NewData)
          break;
        case NotificationType.NotificationResponse:
          notif.finish();
          break;
        case NotificationType.WillPresent:
          notif.finish(WillPresentNotificationResult.All)
          break;
      }
    }
  })
}

const unbind = () => {
  if(notificationListener) notificationListener.remove();
  if(refreshTokenListener) refreshTokenListener.remove();
}

const sendNotification = (token, data) => {
  let body = JSON.stringify({
    "to": token,
    "notification": {
              "title": data.sender || '',
              "body": data. text || '',
              "sound": "default"
      },
    "data": {
      "name": data.sender,
      "chatId": data.chatId,
```

```
      "image": data.image
    },
       "priority": 10
  });

  let headers = new Headers({
               "Content-Type": "application/json",
               "Content-Length": parseInt(body.length),
               "Authorization": "key=" + FirebaseServerKey
  });

  fetch(API_URL, { method: "POST", headers, body })
        .then(response => console.log("Send response", response))
        .catch(error => console.log("Error sending ", error));
}

export default { init, onNotification, sendNotification, unbind }
```

There are four functions exposed in this module:

- `init`: This requests the permission to receive push notifications (in case it was not yet granted) and requests the device token or refreshes it if changed.
- `onNotification`: This invokes a provided callback when a notification is received. In iOS, it also calls the appropriate methods on the notification to close the cycle.
- `unbind`: This stops listening for push notifications.
- `sendNotification`: This formats and sends a push notification to a specific device using a provided notifications token.

Sending notifications in Firebase can be done using their HTTP API, so we will use `fetch` for sending a `POST` request with the proper header and body data.

Now, we have all the logic we need to start building our screens and components.

Login

The `<Login />` component heavily relies on the `users` store for logic, as it is mostly focused on rendering two forms for login and registration. All the validation for the forms is done by Firebase, so we only need to focus on rendering the UI elements and calling the proper store methods.

In this screen, we will be using the `react-native-keyboard-aware-scroll` view, which is a module providing a self-scrolling `<Scrollview />`, which reacts to any focused `<TextInput />` so they are not hidden when the keyboard pops up.

Let's take a look at the code:

```
/*** src/screens/Login.js ***/


import React, { PropTypes } from 'react'
import {
  ScrollView,
  TextInput,
  Button,
  Text,
  View,
  Image,
  ActivityIndicator
} from 'react-native';
import { observer, inject } from 'mobx-react/native'
import Icon from 'react-native-vector-icons/FontAwesome'
import { KeyboardAwareScrollView } from 'react-native-keyboard-aware-
scroll-view'

import LoginForm from '../components/LoginForm'
import RegistrationForm from '../components/RegistrationForm'

@inject('users') @observer
class Login extends React.Component {
  onLogin(email, password) {
    this.props.users.login(email, password);
  }

  onPressRegister(email, password, name) {
    this.props.users.register(email, password, name);
  }

  render() {
    return (
      <KeyboardAwareScrollView style={{padding: 20, marginTop: 20,
        backgroundColor: '#eee'}}>
        <Icon name="comments" size={60} color='#ccc'
          style={{alignSelf: 'center', paddingBottom: 20}}/>
        <View style={{alignItems: 'center', marginBottom: 20}}>
          <Text>- please, login to continue -</Text>
        </View>
        <LoginForm
          onPress={this.onLogin.bind(this)}
```

```
        busy={this.props.users.loggingIn}
        loggingError={this.props.users.loggingError}
      />
      <View style={{alignItems: 'center', marginTop: 20,
                  marginBottom: 20}}>
        <Text>- or register -</Text>
      </View>
      <RegistrationForm
        onPress={this.onPressRegister.bind(this)}
        busy={this.props.users.registering}
        registeringError={this.props.users.registeringError}
      />
    </KeyboardAwareScrollView>
  )
 }
}

export default Login;
```

We split the login screen in two forms: `<LoginForm />` and `<RegistrationForm />`. Both components need to be passed three props:

- `onPress`: What the component needs to do when the `Send` button is pressed.
- `busy`: Are we waiting for remote data?
- `loginError/registrationError`: Description of the error that happened when logging/register (in case it happened).

We are wrapping the whole screen in a `<KeyboardAwareScrollView />` to ensure no `<TextInput />` gets hidden by the keyboard when focused. Let's take a look at the `LoginForm` now:

```
/*** src/components/LoginForm.js ***/

import React, { PropTypes } from 'react'
import {
  TextInput,
  Button,
  Text,
  View,
  Image,
  ActivityIndicator
} from 'react-native';

class LoginForm extends React.Component {
  state= {
    loginEmail: '',
```

```
      loginPassword: ''
  }

onPressLogin() {
  this.props.onPress(this.state.loginEmail,
  this.state.loginPassword);
}

render() {
  return (
      <View style={{backgroundColor: 'white', padding: 15,
                    borderRadius: 10}}>
        {
          this.props.loggingError &&
          <View style={{backgroundColor: '#fcc', borderRadius: 5,
            alignItems: 'center', marginBottom: 10}}>
            <Text>{this.props.loggingError}</Text>
          </View>
        }
        <TextInput
          autoCapitalize='none'
          autoCorrect={false}
          keyboardType='email-address'
          returnKeyType='next'
          style={{height: 40}}
          onChangeText={(loginEmail) => this.setState({loginEmail})}
          value={this.state.loginEmail}
          placeholder='email'
          onSubmitEditing={(event) => {
            this.refs.loginPassword.focus();
          }}
        />
        <TextInput
          ref='loginPassword'
          style={{height: 40}}
          onChangeText={(loginPassword) =>
          this.setState({loginPassword})}
          value={this.state.loginPassword}
          secureTextEntry={true}
          placeholder='password'
        />
        {
          this.props.busy ?
          <ActivityIndicator/>
          :
          <Button
            onPress={this.onPressLogin.bind(this)}
            title='Login'
```

```
                    />
                }
            </View>
        )
    }
}

export default LoginForm;
```

For the `<TextInput />` elements containing the email, we set the
property `keyboardType='email-address'` so the @ sign is easily accessible on the
software keyboard. There are other options such as numeric keyboards, but we will only
use `'email-address'` for this app.

Another useful prop on `<TextInput />` is `returnKeyType`. We
set `returnKeyType='next'` for those form inputs that are not the last ones to display the
`Next` button in the keyboard so the user knows they can go to the next input by tapping
that button. This prop is used in conjunction with a prop like the following:

```
onSubmitEditing={ (event) => {
    this.refs.loginPassword.focus();
}}
```

`onSubmitEditing` is a `<TextInput />` prop that will be invoked when a user presses the
`Return` or `Next` button on the keyboard. We are using it to focus on the next `<TextInput
/>`, which is quite user-friendly when dealing with forms. To get the reference for the next
`<TextInput />` we use `ref`, which is not the safest way, but is good enough for simple
forms. For this to work, we need to assign the corresponding `ref` to the next `<TextInput
/>`: `ref='loginPassword'`.

`RegistrationForm` is a very similar form:

```
/*** src/components/RegistrationForm ***/

import React, { PropTypes } from 'react'
import {
    ScrollView,
    TextInput,
    Button,
    Text,
    View,
    Image,
    ActivityIndicator
} from 'react-native';

class RegisterForm extends React.Component {
```

```
state= {
  registerEmail: '',
  registerPassword: '',
  registerName: ''
}

onPressRegister() {
  this.props.onPress(this.state.registerEmail,
    this.state.registerPassword, this.state.registerName);
}

render() {
  return (
    <View style={{backgroundColor: 'white', padding: 15,
                borderRadius: 10}}>
      {
        this.props.registeringError &&
        <View style={{backgroundColor: '#fcc', borderRadius: 5,
          alignItems: 'center', marginBottom: 10}}>
          <Text>{this.props.registeringError}</Text>
        </View>
      }
      <TextInput
        autoCapitalize='none'
        autoCorrect={false}
        keyboardType='email-address'
        returnKeyType='next'
        style={{height: 40}}
        onChangeText={(registerEmail) =>
        this.setState({registerEmail})}
        value={this.state.registerEmail}
        placeholder='email'
        onSubmitEditing={(event) => {
          this.refs.registerName.focus();
        }}
      />
      <TextInput
        ref='registerName'
        style={{height: 40}}
        onChangeText={(registerName) =>
        this.setState({registerName})}
        returnKeyType='next'
        value={this.state.registerName}
        placeholder='name'
        onSubmitEditing={(event) => {
          this.refs.registerPassword.focus();
        }}
      />
```

```
            <TextInput
              ref='registerPassword'
              style={{height: 40}}
              onChangeText={ (registerPassword) =>
              this.setState({registerPassword})}
              value={this.state.registerPassword}
              secureTextEntry={true}
              placeholder='password'
            />
            {
              this.props.busy ?
              <ActivityIndicator/>
              :
              <Button
                onPress={this.onPressRegister.bind(this)}
                title='Register'
              />
            }
          </View>
        )
      }
    }

    export default RegisterForm;
```

Chats

This is the screen displaying the list of open chats. The special thing to note here is we are using a second navigator to display selected chats on top of the chats list. This means we need a `StackNavigator` in our `Chats` component that will contain two screens: `ChatList` and `Chat`. When a user taps on a chat from `ChatList`, `StackNavigator` will display the selected chat on top of `ChatList` making the list of chats available through a standard `< back` button in the header.

For listing the chats, we will use `<FlatList />`, a performant interface for rendering simple, flat lists, supporting the most of the features from `<ListView />`:

```
/*** src/screens/Chats.js ***/

import React, { PropTypes } from 'react'
import { View, Text, FlatList, ActivityIndicator } from 'react-native'
import { observer, inject } from 'mobx-react/native'
import { StackNavigator } from 'react-navigation'
import Icon from 'react-native-vector-icons/FontAwesome'
import notifications from '../notifications'
```

```
import ListItem from '../components/ListItem'
import Chat from './Chat'

@inject('chats') @observer
class ChatList extends React.Component {
  imgPlaceholder =
  'https://cdn.pixabay.com/photo/2017/03/21/02/00/user-
                 2160923_960_720.png'

  componentWillMount() {
    notifications.onNotification((notif)=>{
      this.props.navigation.goBack();
      this.props.navigation.navigate('Chat', {
        id: notif.chatId,
        name: notif.name || '',
        image: notif.image || this.imgPlaceholder
      })
    });
  }

  render () {
    return (
      <View>
        {
          this.props.chats.list &&
          <FlatList
            data={this.props.chats.list.toJS()}
            keyExtractor={(item, index) => item.id}
            renderItem={({item}) => {
              return (
                <ListItem
                  text={item.name}
                  image={item.image || this.imgPlaceholder}
                  onPress={() => this.props.navigation.navigate('Chat',
                  {
                    id: item.id,
                    name: item.name,
                    image: item.image || this.imgPlaceholder,
                    contactId: item.contactId
                  })}
                />
              )
            }}
          />
        }
        {
          this.props.chats.downloadingChats &&
          <ActivityIndicator style={{marginTop: 20}}/>
```

```
        }
      </View>
    )
  }
}

const Navigator = StackNavigator({
  Chats: {
    screen: ChatList,
    navigationOptions: ({navigation}) => ({
      title: 'Chats',
    }),
  },
  Chat: {
    screen: Chat
  }
});

export default class Chats extends React.Component {
  static navigationOptions = {
    tabBarLabel: 'Chats',
    tabBarIcon: ({ tintColor }) => (
      <Icon name="comment-o" size={30} color={tintColor}/>
    )
  };

  render() {
    return <Navigator />
  }
}
```

The first thing we notice is that we are injecting the `chats` store where the list of chats is saved: `@inject('chats')` `@observer`. We need this to build our `<FlatList />`, based on `this.props.chats.list`, but as the list of chats is an observable MobX object, we need to transform it using its `toJS()` method to make a JavaScript array out of it.

On the `componentWillMount()` function, we will invoke `onNotification` on the notifications module to open the corresponding chat every time the user presses a push notification on her device. Therefore, we will use the `navigate()` method on the navigator to open the proper chat screen including the name of the contact and her avatar.

ListItem

The list of chats relies on `<ListItem />` to render each specific chat within the list. This component is a custom UI class we created to reduce the `ChatList` component complexity:

```
/*** src/components/ListItem.js ***/

import React, { PropTypes } from 'react'
import { View, Image, Text, TouchableOpacity } from 'react-native'
import Icon from 'react-native-vector-icons/FontAwesome'

const ListItem = (props) => {
  return (
    <TouchableOpacity onPress={props.onPress}>
      <View style={{height: 60, borderColor: '#ccc',
                    borderBottomWidth: 1,
          marginLeft: 10, flexDirection: 'row'}}>
        <View style={{padding: 15, paddingTop: 10}}>
          <Image source={{uri: props.image}} style={{width: 40,
                                               height: 40,
            borderRadius: 20, resizeMode: 'cover'}}/>
        </View>
        <View style={{padding: 15, paddingTop: 20}}>
          <Text style={{fontSize: 15}}>{ props.text }</Text>
        </View>
        <Icon name="angle-right" size={20} color="#aaa"
          style={{position: 'absolute', right: 20, top: 20}}/>
      </View>
    </TouchableOpacity>
  )
}

export default ListItem
```

There is little logic on this component as it only receives a prop named `onPress()`, which will be called when the `<ListItem />` is pressed, which, as we saw on this component's parent, will open the chat screen to show the list of messages on that specific chat. Let's take a look at the `chat` screen where all the messages for a specific chat are rendered.

Chat

To keep our code succinct and maintainable, we will use GiftedChat for rendering all the messages in a chat, but there is still some work we need to do to properly render this screen:

```
/*** src/screens/Chat.js ***/

import React, { PropTypes } from 'react'
import { View, Image, ActivityIndicator } from 'react-native';
import { observer, inject } from 'mobx-react/native'
import { GiftedChat } from 'react-native-gifted-chat'

@inject('chats', 'users') @observer
class Chat extends React.Component {
  static navigationOptions = ({ navigation, screenProps }) => ({
    title: navigation.state.params.name,
    headerRight: <Image source={{uri: navigation.state.params.image}}
    style={{
      width: 30,
      height: 30,
      borderRadius: 15,
      marginRight: 10,
      resizeMode: 'cover'
    }}/>
  })

  onSend(messages) {
    this.props.chats.addMessages(this.chatId, this.contactId,
    messages);
  }

  componentWillMount() {
    this.contactId = this.props.navigation.state.params.contactId;
    this.chatId = this.props.navigation.state.params.id;
    this.props.chats.selectChat(this.chatId);
  }

  render () {
    var messages = this.props.chats.selectedChatMessages;
    if(this.props.chats.downloadingChat) {
      return <View><ActivityIndicator style={{marginTop: 20}}/></View>
    }

    return (
      <GiftedChat
        onSend={(messages) => this.onSend(messages)}
        messages={messages ? messages.toJS().reverse() : []}
```

```
        user={{
          _id: this.props.users.id,
          name: this.props.users.name,
          avatar: this.props.users.avatar
        }}
      />
    )
  }
}

export default Chat;
```

We also need to inject some stores for our `<Chat />` component to work. This time, we need `users` and `chats` stores that will be available as props inside the component. This component also expects to receive two params from the navigator: `chatId` (the ID for the chat) and `contactId` (the ID for the person the user is chatting with).

When the component is getting ready to be mounted (`onComponentWillMount()`) we save the `chatId` and `contactId` in more convenient variables inside the component and call the `selectChat()` method on the `chats` store. This will trigger a request to Firebase database to fetch the messages for the selected chat, which will be synced through the `chats` store and is accessible to the component through `this.props.chats.selectedChatMessages`. MobX will also update a `downloadingChat` property to ensure we let the user know the data is being retrieved from Firebase.

Lastly, we need to add a `onSend()` function to `GiftedChat`, which will call the `addMessages()` method on the `chats` store to post the message to Firebase every time the `Send` button is pressed.

`GiftedChat` helped us in largely reducing the amount of work we need to do in order to render the list of messages for a chat. On the other hand, we had to format the messages in the way `GiftedChat` requires and provide an `onSend()` function to be executed whenever we need a message posted to our backend.

Search

The search screen is divided into two parts: a `<TextInput />` for the user to search a name and a `<FlatList />` to show the list of contacts found with the entered name:

```
import React, { PropTypes } from 'react'
import { View, TextInput, Button, FlatList } from 'react-native'
import Icon from 'react-native-vector-icons/FontAwesome'
```

```
import { observer, inject } from 'mobx-react/native'

import ListItem from '../components/ListItem'

@inject('users', 'chats') @observer
class Search extends React.Component {
  imgPlaceholder = 'https://cdn.pixabay.com/photo/2017/03/21/02/00/user-
                   2160923_960_720.png'

  state = {
    name: '',
    foundUsers: null
  }

  static navigationOptions = {
    tabBarLabel: 'Search',
    tabBarIcon: ({ tintColor }) => (
      <Icon name="search" size={30} color={tintColor}/>
    )
  };

  onPressSearch() {
    this.props.users.searchUsers(this.state.name)
    .then((foundUsers) => {
      this.setState({ foundUsers });
    });
  }

  onPressUser(user) {
    //open a chat with the selected user
  }

  render () {
    return (
      <View>
        <View style={{padding: 20, marginTop: 20,
                   backgroundColor: '#eee'}}>
          <View style={{backgroundColor: 'white', padding: 15,
                     borderRadius: 10}}>
            <TextInput
              style={{borderColor: 'gray', borderBottomWidth: 1,
                   height: 40}}
              onChangeText={(name) => this.setState({name})}
              value={this.state.name}
              placeholder='Name of user'
            />
            <Button
              onPress={this.onPressSearch.bind(this)}
```

```
            title='Search'
          />
        </View>
      </View>
      {
        this.state.foundUsers &&
        <FlatList
          data={this.state.foundUsers}
          keyExtractor={(item, index) => index}
          renderItem={({item}) => {
            return (
              <ListItem
                text={item.name}
                image={item.avatar || this.imgPlaceholder}
                onPress={this.onPressUser.bind(this, item)}
              />
            )
          }}
        />
      }
    </View>
  )
  }
}

export default Search;
```

This component requires the injection of both stores (`users` and `chats`). The `users` store is used to invoke the `searchUsers()` method when the user hits the `Search` button. This method doesn't modify the state and therefore we need to provide a callback to receive the list of found users to finally set that list on the component's state.

The second store, `chats`, will be used to store the open chat in Firebase by calling `add()` from the `onPressUser()` function:

```
onPressUser(user) {
  this.props.chats.add({
    id: this.props.users.id,
    name: this.props.users.name,
    avatar: this.props.users.avatar || this.imgPlaceholder,
    notificationsToken: this.props.users.notificationsToken || ''
  }, {
    id: user.id,
    name: user.name,
    avatar: user.avatar || this.imgPlaceholder,
    notificationsToken: user.notificationsToken || ''
  });
```

```
        this.props.navigation.navigate('Chats', {});
    }
```

The add() method in the chats store requires two parameters to be passed: one per each user in the newly open chat. This data will be properly stored in Firebase, so both users will see the chat on their chat list in the app. After adding the new chat, we will navigate the app to the chats screen so the user can see if the addition was successful.

Profile

The profile screen displays the user's avatar, name, and a Logout button for signing out:

```
import React, { PropTypes } from 'react'
import { View, Image, Button, Text } from 'react-native'
import { observer, inject } from 'mobx-react/native'
import Icon from 'react-native-vector-icons/FontAwesome'

import notifications from '../notifications'

@inject('users') @observer
class Profile extends React.Component {
  static navigationOptions = {
    tabBarLabel: 'Profile',
    tabBarIcon: ({ tintColor }) => (
      <Icon name="user" size={30} color={tintColor}/>
    ),
  };

  imgPlaceholder =
  'https://cdn.pixabay.com/photo/2017/03/21/02/00/user-
                    2160923_960_720.png'

  onPressLogout() {
    this.props.users.logout();
  }

  render () {
    return (
        <View style={{ padding: 20 }}>
            {
                this.props.users.name &&
                <View style={{ flexDirection: 'row', alignItems: 'center'
            }}>
                    <Image
                        source={{uri: this.props.users.avatar ||
```

```
                    this.imgPlaceholder}}
                    style={{width: 100, height: 100, borderRadius: 50,
                           margin: 20, resizeMode: 'cover'}}
            />
            <Text style={{fontSize: 25}}>{this.props.users.name}
            </Text>
          </View>
        }
        <Button
          onPress={this.onPressLogout.bind(this)}
          title="Logout"
        />
      </View>
    )
  }
}

export default Profile;
```

The logout process is triggered by calling the `logout()` method on the `users` store. Since we controlled the authentication status in our `src/main.js` file, the app will automatically return to the **Login or Register** screen when the logout is successful.

Summary

We covered several important topics for most of the modern enterprise apps: user management, data synchronization, complex app state, and handling forms. This is a complete app, which we manage to fix with a small code base and the help of MobX and Firebase.

Firebase is very capable of handling this app in production with a large number of users, but building our own backend system should not be a complex task, especially if we have experience in working with `socket.io` and real-time databases.

There are some aspects missing in this chapter such as handling security (which can be done fully within Firebase) or creating chat rooms for more than two users. In any case, these aspects fall out of React Native's environment, so they were intentionally left out.

After finishing this chapter, we should be able to build any app on top of Firebase and MobX as we covered the most used user cases on both pieces of technology. Of course, there are some more complex cases that were left out, but they can be easily learned by having a good understanding of the basics explained throughout this chapter.

In the next chapter, we will build a very different kind of app: a game written in React Native.

7
Game

Most of the most successful apps on the app stores are games. They proved to be really popular as mobile users tend to play all sort of games while commuting, in waiting rooms, when traveling, or even when relaxing at home. It is a fact that mobile users are more inclined to pay for a game than for any other kind of app in the market as the perceived value is higher most of the time.

Modern games are usually built in powerful gaming engines such as Unity or Unreal, as they provide a wide range of tools and frameworks to work with sprites, animations, or physics. But the reality is that great games can also be built in React Native due to its native capabilities. Moreover, React Native has introduced many web and mobile app programmers into game development as it offers them a familiar and intuitive interface. Of course, there are some concepts in game development which need to be understood in order to make the most of the library when building games. Concepts like sprites, ticks, or collisions are small hurdles, which may need to be overcome by non-game developers before building a game.

The game will be built for both iOS and Android, and will use a limited number of external libraries. Redux, the state management library, was chosen to help calculate the position of every sprite on each frame.

We will use some custom sprites and add a sound effect to notice each time the score is increased. One of the main challenges when building a game is making sure the sprites are rendered responsively, so different devices will show the game with the same proportions providing the same game experience across different screen sizes.

This game will be designed to be played in portrait mode only.

Overview

The game we will build in this chapter has simple mechanics:

- The goal is to help a parrot fly between rocks in a cave
- Tapping the screen will result in the parrot flying higher
- Gravity will pull the parrot toward the ground
- Any collision between the parrot and the rocks or the ground will result in the end of the game
- The score will be increased every time the parrot flies through a group of rocks

This kind of game is very well suited to being built with React Native, as it doesn't really need complex animations or physics capabilities. All we need to be sure of is that we move every sprite (graphics component) on the screen at the correct time to create the feeling of continuous animation.

Let's take a look at the initial screen for our game:

This screen presents the logo and instructions about how to get the game started. In this case, a simple tap will start up the game mechanics causing the parrot to fly forward and up on every tap.

The player must help our parrot to fly through the rocks. Each time a set of rocks is passed, the player will get one point.

To make it more difficult, the heights of the rocks will vary forcing the parrot to fly higher or lower to pass through the rocks. If the parrot collides with a rock or the ground, the game will stop and the final score will be presented to the user:

At this point, the user will be able to restart the game by tapping again on the screen.

To make it nicer and easier to play, tapping can be done anywhere on the screen, causing a different effect depending on which screen the user is on:

- On the initial screen tapping will start up the game
- In-game tapping will result in the parrot flying higher
- On the **GAME OVER** screen tapping will restart the game and reset the score

As can be observed, it will be a very simple game but, due to this, easily extendable and fun to play. One import aspect when building this kind of app is counting with a nice set of graphics. For this matter, we will download our assets from one of the multiple game assets markets, which can be found online (most game assets cost a small amount of money although free assets can be found every now and then).

The technical challenges for this game lie more in how the sprites will be moved over time than on a complex state to be maintained. Despite this, we will use Redux to keep and update the app's state as it is a performant and well-known solution. Besides revisiting Redux, we will review the following topics in this chapter:

- Handling animated sprites
- Playing sound effects
- Detecting colliding sprites
- Absolute positioning in different screen resolutions

Sprites

Sprites are the graphics used by the games, normally grouped into one or several images. Many game engines include tools to split and manage those graphics in a convenient way, but this is not the case in React Native. Since it was designed with a different kind of app having in mind, there are several libraries supporting React Native in the task of dealing with sprites, but our game will be simple enough not to need any of these libraries, so we will store one graphic in each image and we will load them separately into the app.

Before starting to build the game, let's get acquainted with the graphics we will load, as they will be the building blocks for the whole app.

Numbers

Instead of using a `<Text />` component to display the score in our game, we will use sprites for a more attractive look. These are the images we will use to represent the user's score:

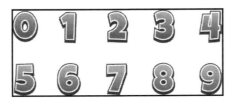

As mentioned, all these graphics will be stored in separate images (named `0.png` to `9.png`) due to React Native's lack of sprite splitting capabilities.

Background

We need a large background to make sure it will fit all screen sizes. In this chapter, we will use this sprite as a static graphic although it could be easily animated to create a nice parallax effect:

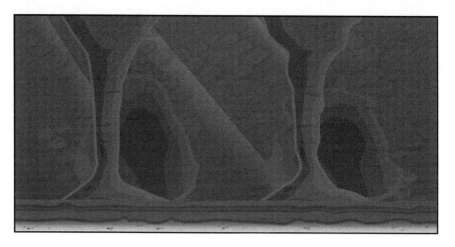

From this background, we will take a piece of ground to animate.

Ground

The ground will be animated in a loop to create a constant feeling of velocity. The size of this image needs to be larger than the maximum screen resolution we want to support, as it should be moved from one side of the screen to the opposite. At all times, two ground images will be displayed, one after the other to ensure at least one of them is shown on the screen during the animation:

Rocks

The moving rocks are the obstacles our parrot needs to pass. There will be one on the top and one on the bottom and both will be animated at the same speed as the ground. Their height will vary for each pair of rocks but always keep the same gap size between them:

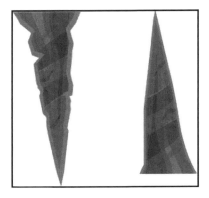

In our `images` folder, we will have `rock-up.png` and `rock-down.png` representing each sprite.

Parrot

We will use two different images for our main character so we can create an animation displaying when the user has tapped on the screen:

The first image will be displayed when the parrot is moving down:

This second image will be shown every time the user presses the screen to move the parrot up. The images will be named `parrot1.png` and `parrot2.png`.

The home screen

For the home screen, we will display two images: a logo and some instructions about how to get the game started. Let's take a look at them:

The instructions to start the game just point out that tapping will get the game started:

Game over screen

When the parrot hits a rock or the ground, the game will end. Then, it is time to display a game over sign and a reset button to get the game started again:

Although the entire screen will be touchable to get the game restarted, we will include a button to let the user know that tapping will result in the game restarting:

This image will be stored as `reset.png`.

This is the full list of images we will have in our game:

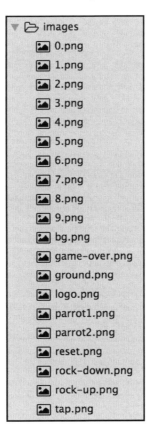

Now, we know the list of images we will use in our game. Let's take a look at the whole folder structure.

Setting up the folder structure

Let's initialize a React Native project using React Native's CLI. The project will be named `birdGame` and will be available for iOS and Android devices:

```
react-native init --version="0.46.4" birdGame
```

As this one is a simple game, we will only need one screen in which we will position all our sprites moving, showing, or hiding them depending on the state of the game, which will be managed by Redux. Therefore, our folder structure will be in line the standard Redux apps:

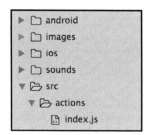

The `actions` folder will only contain one file as there are only three actions which may happen in this game (`start`, `tick`, and `bounce`). There is also a `sounds` folder to store the sound effect which will be played every time the parrot passes a pair of rocks:

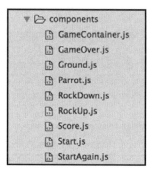

For each sprite, we will create a component so we can move it, show it, or hide it easily:

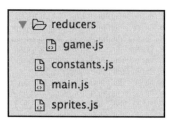

Again, only one reducer will be needed to process all our actions. We will also create two helper files:

- `constants.js`: This is where we will store helper variables for dividing the height and the width of the screen for the device playing the game
- `sprites.js`: This stores all the functions which will calculate how the sprites should be positioned in each frame to create the required animations

`main.js` will serve as the entry point for both iOS and Android and will be responsible to initialize Redux:

The rest of the files are generated by React Native's CLI.

Let's now review the `package.json` file we will need to set the dependencies up in our project:

```
/*** package.json ***/

{
  "name": "birdGame",
  "version": "0.0.1",
  "private": true,
  "scripts": {
    "start": "node node_modules/react-native/local-cli/cli.js start",
    "test": "jest"
  },
  "dependencies": {
    "react": "16.0.0-alpha.12",
    "react-native": "0.46.4",
    "react-native-sound": "^0.10.3",
    "react-redux": "^4.4.5",
    "redux": "^3.5.2"
```

```
  },
  "devDependencies": {
    "babel-jest": "20.0.3",
    "babel-preset-react-native": "2.1.0",
    "jest": "20.0.4",
    "react-test-renderer": "16.0.0-alpha.12"
  },
  "jest": {
    "preset": "react-native"
  }
}
```

Apart from Redux libraries, we will import react-native-sound, which will be in charge of playing any sounds in our game.

After running npm install, we will have our app ready to start coding. As happened in previous apps, the entry point for our messaging app will be the same code both in index.ios.js for iOS and in index.android.js for Android, but both will delegate the initialisation logic to src/main.js:

```
/*** index.ios.js and index.android.js ***/

import { AppRegistry } from 'react-native';
import App from './src/main';

AppRegistry.registerComponent('birdGame', () => App);
```

src/main.js is responsible for initializing Redux and will set GameContainer as the root component in our app:

```
/*** src/main.js ***/

import React from "react";
import { createStore, combineReducers } from "redux";
import { Provider } from "react-redux";

import gameReducer from "./reducers/game";
import GameContainer from "./components/GameContainer";

let store = createStore(combineReducers({ gameReducer }));

export default class App extends React.Component {
  render() {
    return (
      <Provider store={store}>
        <GameContainer />
      </Provider>
```

```
        );
    }
}
```

We use `GameContainer` as the root of the component tree in our app. As a regular Redux app, a `<Provider />` component is in charge of supplying the store to all the components which require reading or modifying the application state.

GameContainer

`GameContainer` is responsible for starting up the game once the user taps the screen. It will do this using `requestAnimationFrame()`--one of the custom timers implemented in React Native.

`requestAnimationFrame()` is similar to `setTimeout()`, but the former will fire after all the frame has flushed, whereas the latter will fire as quickly as possible (over 1000x per second on a iPhone 5S); therefore, `requestAnimationFrame()` is more suited for animated games as it deals only with frames.

As happens with most animated games, we need to create a loop to animate the sprites in the screen by calculating the next position of each element on each frame. This loop will be created by a function named `nextFrame()` inside our `GameContainer`:

```
nextFrame() {
    if (this.props.gameOver) return;
    var elapsedTime = new Date() - this.time;
    this.time = new Date();
    this.props.tick(elapsedTime);
    this.animationFrameId =
      requestAnimationFrame(this.nextFrame.bind(this));
}
```

This function will be aborted if the property `gameOver` is set to `true`. Otherwise, it will trigger the action `tick()` (which calculates how the sprites should be moved on to the next frame, based on the elapsed time) and finally calls itself through `requestAnimationFrame()`. This will keep the loop in the game to animate the moving sprites.

Of course, this nextFrame() should be called at the start for the first time, so we will also create a start() function inside GameContainer to get the game started:

```
start() {
    cancelAnimationFrame(this.animationFrameId);
    this.props.start();
    this.props.bounce();
    this.time = new Date();
    this.setState({ gameOver: false });
    this.animationFrameId =
        requestAnimationFrame(this.nextFrame.bind(this));
}
```

The start function makes sure there is no animation started by calling cancelAnimationFrame(). This will prevent any double animations being performed when the user resets the game.

Then, the functions trigger the start() action, which will just set a flag in the store to notice the game has started.

We want to start the game by moving the parrot up, so the user has the time to react. For this, we also call the bounce() action.

Finally, we start the animation loop by passing the already known nextFrame() function as a callback of requestAnimationFrame().

Let's also review the render() method we will use for this container:

```
render() {
    const {
        rockUp,
        rockDown,
        ground,
        ground2,
        parrot,
        isStarted,
        gameOver,
        bounce,
        score
    } = this.props;

    return (
        <TouchableOpacity
            onPress={
                !isStarted || gameOver ? this.start.bind(this) :
                    bounce.bind(this)
            }
```

```
    style={styles.screen}
    activeOpacity={1}
  >
    <Image
      source={require("../../images/bg.png")}
      style={[styles.screen, styles.image]}
    />
    <RockUp
      x={rockUp.position.x * W} //W is a responsiveness factor
                               //explained in the 'constants' section
      y={rockUp.position.y}
      height={rockUp.size.height}
      width={rockUp.size.width}
    />
    <Ground
      x={ground.position.x * W}
      y={ground.position.y}
      height={ground.size.height}
      width={ground.size.width}
    />
    <Ground
      x={ground2.position.x * W}
      y={ground2.position.y}
      height={ground2.size.height}
      width={ground2.size.width}
    />
    <RockDown
      x={rockDown.position.x * W}
      y={rockDown.position.y * H} //H is a responsiveness factor
                                 //explained in the 'constants'
                                 //section
      height={rockDown.size.height}
      width={rockDown.size.width}
    />
    <Parrot
      x={parrot.position.x * W}
      y={parrot.position.y * H}
      height={parrot.size.height}
      width={parrot.size.width}
    />
    <Score score={score} />
    {!isStarted && <Start />}
    {gameOver && <GameOver />}
    {gameOver && isStarted && <StartAgain />}
  </TouchableOpacity>
);
}
```

It may be lengthy, but actually, it's a simple positioning of all the visible elements on the screen while wrapping them in a `<TouchableOpacity />` component to capture the user tapping no matter in which part of the screen. This `<TouchableOpacity />` component is actually not sending any feedback to the user when they tap the screen (we disabled it by passing `activeOpacity={1}` as a prop) since this feedback is already provided by the parrot bouncing on each tap.

 We could have used React Native's `<TouchableWithoutFeedback />` for this matter, but it has several limitations which would have harmed our performance.

The provided `onPress` attribute just defines what the app should do when the user taps on the screen:

- If the game is active, it will bounce the parrot sprite
- If the user is on the game over screen it will restart the game by calling the `start()` action

All other children in the `render()` method are the graphic elements in our game, specifying for each of them, their position and size. It's also important to note several points:

- There are two `<Ground />` components because we need to continuously animate it in the *x* axis. They will be positioned one after the other horizontally to animate them together so when the end of the first `<Ground />` component is shown on screen, the beginning of the second will follow creating the sense of continuum.
- The background is not contained in any custom component but in `<Image />`. This is because it doesn't need any special logic being a static element.
- Some positions are multiplied by factor variables (W and H). We will take a deeper look at these variables in the constants section. At this point, we only need to know that they are variables helping in the absolute positioning of the elements taking into account all screen sizes.

Let's now put all these functions together to build up our `<GameContainer />`:

```
/*** src/components/GameContainer.js ***/

import React, { Component } from "react";
import { connect } from "react-redux";
import { bindActionCreators } from "redux";
```

```javascript
import { TouchableOpacity, Image, StyleSheet } from "react-native";

import * as Actions from "../actions";
import { W, H } from "../constants";
import Parrot from "./Parrot";
import Ground from "./Ground";
import RockUp from "./RockUp";
import RockDown from "./RockDown";
import Score from "./Score";
import Start from "./Start";
import StartAgain from "./StartAgain";
import GameOver from "./GameOver";

class Game extends Component {
  constructor() {
    super();
    this.animationFrameId = null;
    this.time = new Date();
  }

  nextFrame() {
    ...
  }

  start() {
    ...
  }

  componentWillUpdate(nextProps, nextState) {
    if (nextProps.gameOver) {
      this.setState({ gameOver: true });
      cancelAnimationFrame(this.animationFrameId);
    }
  }

  shouldComponentUpdate(nextProps, nextState) {
    return !nextState.gameOver;
  }

  render() {
    ...

  }
}

const styles = StyleSheet.create({
  screen: {
    flex: 1,
```

```
      alignSelf: "stretch",
      width: null
    },
    image: {
      resizeMode: "cover"
    }
  });

  function mapStateToProps(state) {
    const sprites = state.gameReducer.sprites;
    return {
      parrot: sprites[0],
      rockUp: sprites[1],
      rockDown: sprites[2],
      gap: sprites[3],
      ground: sprites[4],
      ground2: sprites[5],
      score: state.gameReducer.score,
      gameOver: state.gameReducer.gameOver,
      isStarted: state.gameReducer.isStarted
    };
  }
  function mapStateActionsToProps(dispatch) {
    return bindActionCreators(Actions, dispatch);
  }

  export default connect(mapStateToProps, mapStateActionsToProps)(Game);
```

We added three more ES6 and React lifecycle methods to this component:

- super(): The constructor will save an attribute named animationFrameId to
  capture the ID for the animation frame in which the nextFrame function will run
  and also another attribute named time will store the exact time at which the
  game was initialized. This time attribute will be used by the tick() function to
  calculate how much the sprites should be moved.
- componentWillUpdate(): This function will be called every time new props
  (positions and sizes for the sprites in the game) are passed. It will detect when the
  game must be stopped due to a collision so the game over screen will be
  displayed.
- shouldComponentUpdate(): This performs another check to avoid re-rendering
  the game container if the game has ended.

The rest of the functions are Redux related. They are in charge of connecting the component to the store by injecting actions and attributes:

- mapStateToProps(): This gets the data for all the sprites in the store and injects them into the component as props. The sprites will be stored in an array and therefore they will be accessed by index. On top of these, the Score, a flag noting if the current game is over, and a flag noting if the game is in progress will also be retrieved from the state and injected into the component.
- mapStateActionsToProps(): This will inject the three available actions (tick, bounce, and start) into the component so they can be used by it.

 Accessing the sprites data by index is not a recommended practice as indexes can change if the number of sprites grows, but we will use it like this in this app for simplicity reasons.

Actions

As we mentioned before, only three Redux actions will be available:

- tick(): To calculate the next position of the sprites on the screen
- bounce(): To make the parrot fly up
- start(): To initialize the game variables

This means our src/actions/index.js file should be very simple:

```
/*** src/actions/index.js ***/

export function start() {
  return { type: "START" };
}

export function tick(elapsedTime) {
  return { type: "TICK", elapsedTime };
}

export function bounce() {
  return { type: "BOUNCE" };
}
```

Only the `tick()` action needs to pass a payload: the time it passed since the last frame.

Reducer

Since we have a very limited amount of actions, our reducer will also be fairly simple and will delegate most of the functionality to the sprites helper functions in the `src/sprites.js` file:

```
/*** src/reducers/index.js ***/

import {
  sprites,
  moveSprites,
  checkForCollision,
  getUpdatedScore,
  bounceParrot
} from "../sprites";

const initialState = {
  score: 0,
  gameOver: false,
  isStarted: false,
  sprites
};

export default (state = initialState, action) => {
  switch (action.type) {
    case "TICK":
      return {
        ...state,
        sprites: moveSprites(state.sprites, action.elapsedTime),
        gameOver: checkForCollision(state.sprites[0],
        state.sprites.slice(1)),
        score: getUpdatedScore(state.sprites, state.score)
      };
    case "BOUNCE":
      return {
        ...state,
        sprites: bounceParrot(state.sprites)
      };
    case "START":
      return {
        ...initialState,
        isStarted: true
      };
```

```
      default:
         return state;
   }
};
```

The `start()` function only needs to set the `isStarted` flag to `true`, as the initial state will have it set to `false` by default. We will reuse this initial state every time the game ends.

`bounce()` will use the `bounceParrot()` function from the sprites module to set a new direction for the main character.

The most important changes will happen when the `tick()` function is triggered, as it needs to calculate the positions of all moving elements (through the `moveSprites()` function), detect if the parrot has collided with any static elements (through the `checkForCollision()` function), and update the score in the store (through the `getUpdatedScore()` function).

As we can see, most of the game's functionality is delegated to the helper functions inside the sprites module, so let's take a deeper look into the `src/sprites.js` file.

The sprites module

The structure of the sprites module is formed by an array of sprites and several exported functions:

```
/*** src/sprites.js ***/

import sound from "react-native-sound";

const coinSound = new sound("coin.wav", sound.MAIN_BUNDLE);
let heightOfRockUp = 25;
let heightOfRockDown = 25;
let heightOfGap = 30;
let heightOfGround = 20;

export const sprites = [
   ...
];

function prepareNewRockSizes() {
   ...
}

function getRockProps(type) {
```

```
    . . .
}

export function moveSprites(sprites, elapsedTime = 1000 / 60) {
    . . .
}

export function bounceParrot(sprites) {
    . . .
}

function hasCollided(mainSprite, sprite) {
    . . .
}

export function checkForCollision(mainSprite, sprites) {
    . . .
}

export function getUpdatedScore(sprites, score) {
    . . .
}
```

This module begins by loading the sound effect we will play when the parrot passes a set of rocks to give feedback to the user about the increment in their score.

Then, we define some heights for several sprites:

- heightOfRockUp: This is the height of the rock which will appear in the upper part of the screen.
- heightOfRockDown: This is the height of the rock which will show in the lower part of the screen.
- heightOfGap: We will create an invisible view between the upper and the lower rock to detect when the parrot has passed each set of rocks so the score is updated. This this gap's height.
- heightOfGround: This is a static value for the height of the ground.

Each other item in this module plays a role in moving or positioning the sprites on the screen.

The sprites array

This is the array in charge of storing all the sprite's positions and sizes at a given time. Why are we using an array for storing our sprites instead of a hash map (Object)? Mainly for extensibility; Although a hash map would make our code noticeably more readable, if we want to add new sprites of an existing type (as it happens with the `ground` sprite in this app) we would need to use artificial keys for each of them despite being the same type. Using an array of sprites is a recurrent pattern in game development which allows to decouple the implementation from the list of sprites.

Whenever we want to move a sprite, we will update its position in this array:

```
export const sprites = [
  {
    type: "parrot",
    position: { x: 50, y: 55 },
    velocity: { x: 0, y: 0 },
    size: { width: 10, height: 8 }
  },
  {
    type: "rockUp",
    position: { x: 110, y: 0 },
    velocity: { x: -1, y: 0 },
    size: { width: 15, height: heightOfRockUp }
  },
  {
    type: "rockDown",
    position: { x: 110, y: heightOfRockUp + 30 },
    velocity: { x: -1, y: 0 },
    size: { width: 15, height: heightOfRockDown }
  },
  {
    type: "gap",
    position: { x: 110, y: heightOfRockUp },
    velocity: { x: -1, y: 0 },
    size: { width: 15, height: 30 }
  },
  {
    type: "ground",
    position: { x: 0, y: 80 },
    velocity: { x: -1, y: 0 },
    size: { width: 100, height: heightOfGround }
  },
  {
    type: "ground",
    position: { x: 100, y: 80 },
```

```
      velocity: { x: -1, y: 0 },
      size: { width: 100, height: heightOfGround }
    }
  ];
```

The array will store the initial values for positioning and sizing all the moving sprites in the game.

prepareNewRockSizes()

This function randomly calculates the size of the next upper and lower rock together with the height of the gap between them:

```
function prepareNewRockSizes() {
  heightOfRockUp = 10 + Math.floor(Math.random() * 40);
  heightOfRockDown = 50 - heightOfRockUp;
  heightOfGap = 30;
}
```

It's important to note that this function only calculates the heights for the new set of rocks but doesn't create them. This is just a preparation step.

getRockProps()

The helper functions to format the position and size attributes of a rock (or gap):

```
function getRockProps(type) {
  switch (type) {
    case "rockUp":
      return { y: 0, height: heightOfRockUp };
    case "rockDown":
      return { y: heightOfRockUp + heightOfGap,
               height: heightOfRockDown };
    case "gap":
      return { y: heightOfRockUp, height: heightOfGap };
  }
}
```

moveSprites()

This is the main function as it calculates the new position for each sprite stored in the sprites array. Game development relies in physics to calculate the position for each sprite in each frame.

For example, if we want to move an object to the right side of the screen, we will need to update its x position a number of pixels. The more pixels we add to the object's x attribute for the next frame, the faster it will move (`sprite.x = sprite.x + 5;` moves `sprite` five times faster than `sprite.x = sprite.x + 1;`).

As we can see in the following example, the way we calculate the new position for each sprite is based on three factors: the current position of the sprite, the time that has passed since the last frame (`elapsedTime`), and the gravity/velocity of the sprite (`i.e.` `sprite.velocity.y + elapsedTime * gravity`).

Additionally, we will use the helper function `getRockProps` to get the new sizes and positions for the rocks. Let's take a look at how the `moveSprites` function looks like:

```
export function moveSprites(sprites, elapsedTime = 1000 / 60) {
  const gravity = 0.0001;
  let newSprites = [];

  sprites.forEach(sprite => {
    if (sprite.type === "parrot") {
      var newParrot = {
        ...sprite,
        position: {
          x: sprite.position.x,
          y:
            sprite.position.y +
            sprite.velocity.y * elapsedTime +
            0.5 * gravity * elapsedTime * elapsedTime
        },
        velocity: {
          x: sprite.velocity.x,
          y: sprite.velocity.y + elapsedTime * gravity
        }
      };
      newSprites.push(newParrot);
    } else if (
      sprite.type === "rockUp" ||
      sprite.type === "rockDown" ||
      sprite.type === "gap"
    ) {
```

```
        let rockPosition,
          rockSize = sprite.size;
        if (sprite.position.x > 0 - sprite.size.width) {
          rockPosition = {
            x: sprite.position.x + sprite.velocity.x,
            y: sprite.position.y
          };
        } else {
          rockPosition = { x: 100, y: getRockProps(sprite.type).y };
          rockSize = { width: 15,
                       height: getRockProps(sprite.type).height };
        }
        var newRock = {
          ...sprite,
          position: rockPosition,
          size: rockSize
        };
        newSprites.push(newRock);
      } else if (sprite.type === "ground") {
        let groundPosition;
        if (sprite.position.x > -97) {
          groundPosition = { x: sprite.position.x + sprite.velocity.x,
                             y: 80 };
        } else {
          groundPosition = { x: 100, y: 80 };
        }
        var newGround = { ...sprite, position: groundPosition };
        newSprites.push(newGround);
      }
    });
    return newSprites;
  }
```

Calculating the next position for a sprite is, most of the time, basic addition (or subtraction). Let's take, for example, how the parrot should move:

```
var newParrot = {
        ...sprite,
        position: {
          x: sprite.position.x,
          y:
            sprite.position.y +
            sprite.velocity.y * elapsedTime +
            0.5 * gravity * elapsedTime * elapsedTime
        },
        velocity: {
          x: sprite.velocity.x,
```

```
          y: sprite.velocity.y + elapsedTime * gravity
     }
  }
```

The parrot will only move vertically, basing its speed on gravity, so the x attribute will always stay fixed for it while the y attribute will change according to the function `sprite.position.y + sprite.velocity.y * elapsedTime + 0.5 * gravity * elapsedTime * elapsedTime` which, in summary, adds the elapsed time and the gravity in different factors.

The calculations for how the rocks should move are a little more complex, as we need to take into account every time the rocks disappear from the screen (`if (sprite.position.x > 0 - sprite.size.width)`). As they have been passed, we need to recreate them with different heights (`rockPosition = { x: 100, y: getRockProps(sprite.type).y }`).

We have the same behavior for the ground, in terms of having to recreate it once it abandons the screen completely (`if (sprite.position.x > -97)`).

bounceParrot()

The only task for this function is changing the velocity of the main character, so it will fly up reversing the effect of gravity. This function will be called whenever the user taps on the screen while the game is started:

```
export function bounceParrot(sprites) {
  var newSprites = [];
  var sprite = sprites[0];
  var newParrot = { ...sprite, velocity: { x: sprite.velocity.x,
                  y: -0.05 } };
  newSprites.push(newParrot);
  return newSprites.concat(sprites.slice(1));
}
```

It's a simple operation in which we take the parrot's sprite data from the `sprites` array; we change its velocity on the *y* axis to a negative value so that the parrot moves upwards.

checkForCollision()

checkForCollision() is responsible for identifying if any of the rigid sprites have collided with the parrot sprite, so the game can be stopped. It will use hasCollided() as a supporting function to perform the required calculations on each specific sprite:

```
function hasCollided(mainSprite, sprite) {
  /***
   *** we will check if 'mainSprite' has entered in the
   *** space occupied by 'sprite' by comparing their
   *** position, width and height
   ***/

  var mainX = mainSprite.position.x;
  var mainY = mainSprite.position.y;
  var mainWidth = mainSprite.size.width;
  var mainHeight = mainSprite.size.height;

  var spriteX = sprite.position.x;
  var spriteY = sprite.position.y;
  var spriteWidth = sprite.size.width;
  var spriteHeight = sprite.size.height;

  /***
   *** this if statement checks if any border of mainSprite
   *** sits within the area covered by sprite
   ***/

  if (
    mainX < spriteX + spriteWidth &&
    mainX + mainWidth > spriteX &&
    mainY < spriteY + spriteHeight &&
    mainHeight + mainY > spriteY
  ) {
    return true;
  }
}

export function checkForCollision(mainSprite, sprites) {
  /***
   *** loop through all sprites in the sprites array
   *** checking, for each of them, if there is a
   *** collision with the mainSprite (parrot)
   ***/

  return sprites.filter(sprite => sprite.type !== "gap").find(sprite => {
```

```
            return hasCollided(mainSprite, sprite);
    });
}
```

For simplicity, we assume that all sprites have a rectangular shape (even though rocks grow thinner towards the end) because the calculation would be a lot more complex if we considered different shapes.

In summary, checkForCollision() is just looping through the sprites array to find any colliding sprite, hasCollided() checks for collisions based on the sprite size and position. In just an if statement, we compare the boundaries of a sprite and the parrot's sprite to see if any of those boundaries are occupying the same area of the screen.

getUpdatedScore()

The last function in the sprites module will check if the score needs to be updated based on parrot position relative to the gap position (the gap between the upper and the lower rock is also counted as a sprite):

```
export function getUpdatedScore(sprites, score) {
    var parrot = sprites[0];
    var gap = sprites[3];

    var parrotXPostion = parrot.position.x;
    var gapXPosition = gap.position.x;
    var gapWidth = gap.size.width;

    if (parrotXPostion === gapXPosition + gapWidth) {
        coinSound.play();
        score++;
        prepareNewRockSizes();
    }

    return score;
}
```

An if statement checks if the parrot's position in the *x* axis has surpassed the gap (gapXPosition + gapWidth). When this happens, we play the sound we created in the header of the module (const coinSound = new sound("coin.wav", sound.MAIN_BUNDLE);) by calling its play() method. Moreover, we will increase the score variable and prepare a new set of rocks to be rendered when the current ones leave the screen.

Constants

We already saw the variables w and H. They represent one part of the screen if we divided it into 100 parts. Let's take a look at the `constants.js` file to understand this better:

```
/*** src/constants.js ***/

import { Dimensions } from "react-native";

var { width, height } = Dimensions.get("window");

export const W = width / 100;
export const H = height / 100;
```

W can be calculated as the total width of the device's screen divided by 100 units (as percentages are easier to reason about when positioning our sprites). The same goes for H; it can be calculated by dividing the total height by 100. Using these two constants, we can position and size our sprites relative to the size of the screen, so all screen sizes will display the same ratios for positions and sizes.

These constants will be used in all the visual components requiring responsive capabilities so they will show and move different depending on the screen size. This technique will ensure the game is playable even in small screens as the sprites will be resized accordingly.

Let's move on now to the components which will be displayed inside the <GameContainer />.

Parrot

The main character will be represented by this component, which will comprise of two different images (the same parrot with its wings up and down) driven by the Y position property passed by <GameContainer />:

```
/*** src/components/parrot.js ***/

import React from "react";
import { Image } from "react-native";
import { W, H } from "../constants";

export default class Parrot extends React.Component {
  constructor() {
    super();
    this.state = { wings: "down" };
```

```
  }

  componentWillUpdate(nextProps, nextState) {
    if (this.props.y < nextProps.y) {
      this.setState({ wings: "up" });
    } else if (this.props.y > nextProps.y) {
      this.setState({ wings: "down" });
    }
  }

  render() {
    let parrotImage;
    if (this.state.wings === "up") {
      parrotImage = require("../../images/parrot1.png");
    } else {
      parrotImage = require("../../images/parrot2.png");
    }
    return (
      <Image
        source={parrotImage}
        style={{
          position: "absolute",
          resizeMode: "contain",
          left: this.props.x,
          top: this.props.y,
          width: 12 * W,
          height: 12 * W
        }}
      />
    );
  }
}
```

We use a state variable named `wings` to pick which image the parrot will be--when it is flying up the image with the wings down will be displayed while the wings up will be shown when flying down. The way this will be calculated is based on the position of the bird on the *y* axis passed as a property from the container:

- If the Y position is lower than the previous Y position means the bird is going down and therefore the wings should be up
- If the Y position is higher than the previous Y position means the bird is going up and therefore the wings should be down

The size of the parrot is fixed to `12 * W` both for the `height` and `width` as the sprite is a square and we want it to be sized relative to the width of each screen device.

RockUp and RockDown

The sprites for the rocks have no logic on them and are basically <Image /> components positioned and sized by the parent component. This is the code for <RockUp />:

```
/*** src/components/RockUp.js ***/

import React, { Component } from "react";
import { Image } from "react-native";

import { W, H } from "../constants";

export default class RockUp extends Component {
  render() {
    return (
      <Image
        resizeMode="stretch"
        source={require("../../images/rock-down.png")}
        style={{
          position: "absolute",
          left: this.props.x,
          top: this.props.y,
          width: this.props.width * W,
          height: this.props.height * H
        }}
      />
    );
  }
}
```

The height and the width will be calculated by the following formulae: `this.props.width * W` and `this.props.height * H`. This will size the rock relative to the device's screen and the provided height and width.

The code for <RockDown /> is quite similar:

```
/*** src/components/RockDown.js ***/

import React, { Component } from "react";
import { Image } from "react-native";

import { W, H } from "../constants";

export default class RockDown extends Component {
  render() {
    return (
```

```
    <Image
      resizeMode="stretch"
      source={require("../../images/rock-up.png")}
      style={{
        position: "absolute",
        left: this.props.x,
        top: this.props.y,
        width: this.props.width * W,
        height: this.props.height * H
      }}
    />
  );
}
}
```

Ground

Building the ground component is similar to the rock sprites. An image rendered in the proper position and size will be sufficient for this component:

```
/*** src/components/Ground.js ***/

import React, { Component } from "react";
import { Image } from "react-native";

import { W, H } from "../constants";

export default class Ground extends Component {
  render() {
    return (
      <Image
        resizeMode="stretch"
        source={require("../../images/ground.png")}
        style={{
          position: "absolute",
          left: this.props.x,
          top: this.props.y * H,
          width: this.props.width * W,
          height: this.props.height * H
        }}
      />
    );
  }
}
```

In this case, we will use H to relatively positioning the ground image.

Score

We decided to use number images to render the score, so we will need to load them and pick the appropriate digits depending on the user's score:

```
/*** src/components/Score.js ***/

import React, { Component } from "react";
import { View, Image } from "react-native";

import { W, H } from "../constants";

export default class Score extends Component {
  getSource(num) {
    switch (num) {
      case "0":
        return require("../../images/0.png");
      case "1":
        return require("../../images/1.png");
      case "2":
        return require("../../images/2.png");
      case "3":
        return require("../../images/3.png");
      case "4":
        return require("../../images/4.png");
      case "5":
        return require("../../images/5.png");
      case "6":
        return require("../../images/6.png");
      case "7":
        return require("../../images/7.png");
      case "8":
        return require("../../images/8.png");
      case "9":
        return require("../../images/9.png");
      default:
        return require("../../images/0.png");
    }
  }

  render() {
    var scoreString = this.props.score.toString();
    var scoreArray = [];
    for (var index = 0; index < scoreString.length; index++) {
      scoreArray.push(scoreString[index]);
    }
```

```
    return (
      <View
        style={{
          position: "absolute",
          left: 47 * W,
          top: 10 * H,
          flexDirection: "row"
        }}
      >
        {scoreArray.map(
          function(item, i) {
            return (
              <Image
                style={{ width: 10 * W }}
                key={i}
                resizeMode="contain"
                source={this.getSource(item)}
              />
            );
          }.bind(this)
        )}
      </View>
    );
  }
}
```

We are doing the following in the `render` method:

- Converting the score to a string
- Converting the string into a list of digits
- Turning this list of digits into a list of images using the supporting `getSource()` function

One of the limitations in React Native `<Image />` is that its source cannot be required as a variable. Hence, we are using this small trick of retrieving the source from our `getSource()` method, which actually acquires all the possible images and returns the correct one through a `switch`/`case` clause.

Start

The start screen includes two images:

- A logo
- A start button explaining how to start up the game (tapping anywhere on the screen)

```
/*** src/components/Start.js ***/

import React, { Component } from "react";
import { Text, View, StyleSheet, Image } from "react-native";

import { W, H } from "../constants";

export default class Start extends Component {
  render() {
    return (
      <View style={{ position: "absolute", left: 20 * W, top: 3 * H }}>
        <Image
          resizeMode="contain"
          source={require("../../images/logo.png")}
          style={{ width: 60 * W }}
        />
        <Image
          resizeMode="contain"
          style={{ marginTop: 15, width: 60 * W }}
          source={require("../../images/tap.png")}
        />
      </View>
    );
  }
}
```

We are using our H and W constants again to ensure the elements are positioned in the right place on every device screen.

GameOver

When the parrot collides with a rock or the ground, we should display the game over screen. This screen only contains two images:

- A game over sign
- A button to restart the game

Let's first take a look at the game over sign:

```
/*** src/components/GameOver.js ***/

import React, { Component } from "react";
import { Image } from "react-native";

import { W, H } from "../constants";

export default class GameOver extends Component {
  render() {
    return (
      <Image
        style={{
          position: "absolute",
          left: 15 * W,
          top: 30 * H
        }}
        resizeMode="stretch"
        source={require("../../images/game-over.png")}
      />
    );
  }
}
```

Now, let's move on to the reset the game button.

StartAgain

Actually, the reset button is only a sign as the user will be able to tap not only on the button but anywhere on the screen to get the game started. In any case, we will position this button properly on every screen using the H and W constants:

```
/*** src/components/StartAgain.js ***/

import React, { Component } from "react";
import { Text, View, StyleSheet, TouchableOpacity, Image }
from "react-native";

import { W, H } from "../constants";

export default class StartAgain extends Component {
  render() {
    return (
      <Image
        style={{ position: "absolute", left: 35 * W, top: 40 * H }}
```

```
            resizeMode="contain"
            source={require("../../images/reset.png")}
          />
        );
      }
    }
```

Summary

Games are a very special kind of app. They are based on displaying and moving sprites on the screen, depending on the time and the user interaction. That is why we spent most of this chapter explaining how we could easily display all the images in the most performant way and how to position and size them.

We also reviewed a common trick to position and size sprites relatively to the height and width of the device screen.

Despite not being designed for games specifically, Redux was used to store and distribute the sprite's data around the components in our app.

At a general level, we proved that React Native can be used to build performant games and, although it lacks game-specific tooling, we can produce a very readable code which means it should be easy to extend and maintain. In fact, some very easy extensions can be created at this stage to make the game more fun and playable: increase speed after passing a specific amount of obstacles, reduce or increase the gap size, show more than one set of rocks on screen at once, etc.

The next chapter will review the blueprint of a more conventional type of app: an e-commerce app.

8
E-Commerce App

Online shopping is something most retailers have adopted, but users are slowly migrating from websites to mobile apps. That's why e-commerce has set a strong focus on responsive websites, which can be seamlessly accessed from a desktop computer or a mobile browser. Along with that, users also demand higher standards of quality which cannot always be met by even the most responsive websites. Loading times, laggy animations, non-native components, or a lack of native features may hurt user experiences resulting in low conversion rates.

Building our e-commerce app in React Native can reduce the development efforts required due to the possibility of reusing some web components, which were already designed for the web (using React.js). Besides that, we can reduce the time to market and development costs, making React Native a very attractive tool for small and medium-sized businesses willing to sell their products or services online.

In this chapter, we will focus on building a bookstore for iOS and Android reusing 100% of our code. Despite focusing on a bookstore, the same codebase could be reused to sell any kind of products just by replacing the products list.

To free us from building an API for this app, we will mock all the data behind a fake API service. The state management library we will use for this app will be Redux and its middleware `redux-thunk` to handle asynchronous calls.

Asynchronous calls and redux-thunk were already explained in Chapter 4, *Image Sharing App*. It may be useful to review its usage in that chapter to reinforce the main concepts before moving into the Actions sections in this chapter.

Navigation will be handled by `react-navigation` as it is the most complete and performant navigation library in React Native developed to date. Finally, we will use some very useful libraries, especially for e-commerce apps, such as `react-native-credit-card-input`, which handles credit card inputs.

While building this app, we will emphasize several quality aspects to make sure the app is production-ready by the end of the chapter. For example, we will use type validation extensively for properties and code linting.

Overview

Instead of putting much effort into the app's look and feel, as we did in previous chapters, we will focus on functionality and code quality for this one. Nevertheless, we will build it in a way which will allow any developer to style it easily at a later stage. With that in mind, let's take a look at what the app will look like once finished.

Let's start from the home screen where all the books are displayed:

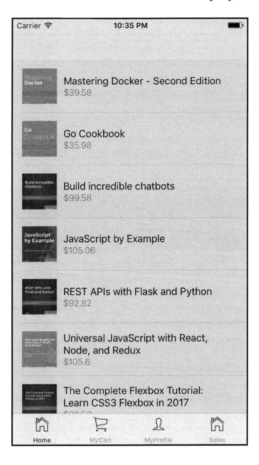

In Android, we will add a drawer navigation pattern instead of a tabbed one as Android users are more used to it:

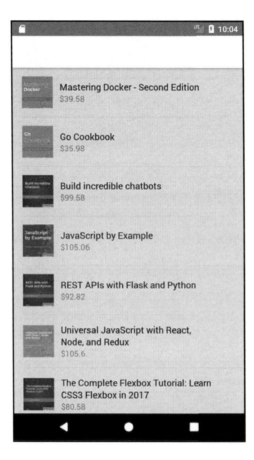

The drawer can be opened by swiping the screen from the left edge to the right:

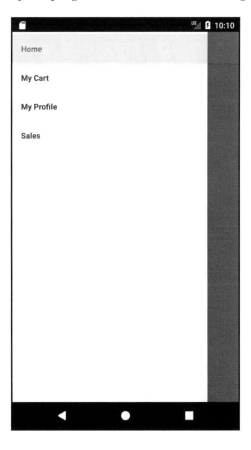

Now, let's see what happens when a user taps on one of the books from the home screen (list of books available):

The Android version for this screen will be similar, as only a couple of native components will adopt a different styling, depending on which platform the app is executed:

Only logged-in users will be able to buy books from our app. This means that we need to pop up a login/registration screen at a certain point, and clicking on the **BUY!** button seems like an appropriate moment for this:

In this case, the Android version will look different from the iOS because of the difference in styles between native buttons on each platform:

For testing purposes, we created a test account in this app with the following credentials:

- **e-mail**: test@test.com
- **password**: test

In case the user still doesn't have an account, she will be able to click on the **OR REGISTER** button to create one:

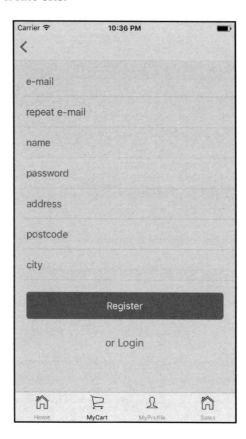

This form will include the following validations:

- **e-mail** and **repeat e-mail** field values match
- All the fields are entered

In case any of these validations fail, we will display an error message at the bottom of this screen:

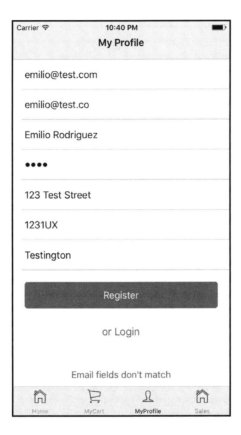

After registering, the user will be logged in automatically and will be able to continue her purchase journey by reviewing her cart:

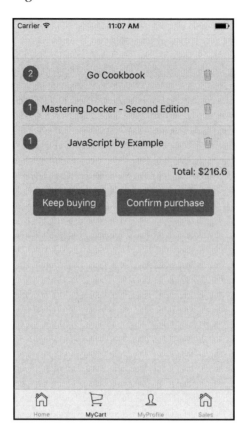

Again, the Android version will show small differences in the looks of this screen:

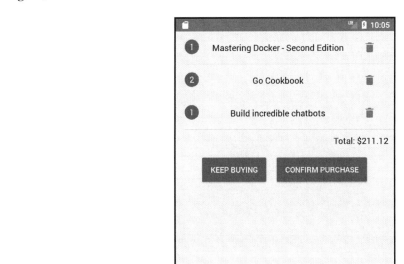

By clicking on the **KEEP BUYING** button on this screen, the user will be sent back to the home screen where all the available books are displayed for her to continue adding items to her cart.

In case she decides to confirm her purchase, the app will display a payment screen in which the user can enter her credit card details:

The **Pay now** button will only be active when all the data has been entered correctly:

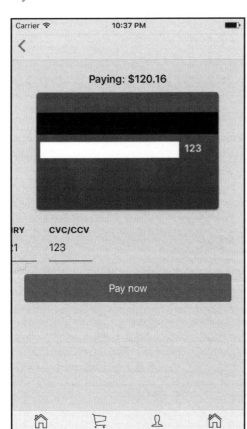

For testing purposes, the developers can use the following credit card data:

- **Card number**: 4111 1111 1111 1111
- **Date of expiration**: any date in the future
- **CVC/CVV**: 123

Once the payment has gone through, the user will receive a confirmation of her purchase detailing all the items which will be sent to her address:

This screen will finish the purchase journey. At this stage, the user can click on the **Continue Shopping** button to go back to the list of available products.

There are two more journeys available through the tabbed/drawer navigation. The first one is to the **My Profile** section to review her account details or **Logout**:

If the user still didn't log in, the app will show the login/register form on this screen.

The last journey is accessed through the **Sales** tab/menu item:

By pressing **Add to cart**, the user will be sent directly to the purchase journey where she can add more items to the cart or directly confirm the purchase by entering her login (if not present) and payment details.

Lastly, every time we need to receive data from the backend API, we will display a spinner to let the user know there is some activity happening in the background:

Since we will mock all the API calls, we will need to add a small delay to their responses in order to see the spinners, so the developers can have a similar experience as users will have, when we replace the mocked up calls for real API requests.

Setting up the folder structure

This app will use Redux, as its state management library, which will define the folder structure we will be using throughout this chapter. Let's start by initializing the project through React Native's CLI:

```
react-native init --version="0.48.3" ecommerce
```

As we have seen in previous chapters where we used Redux, we need our folder structure to accommodate different module types:
`reducers`, `actions`, `components`, `screens`, and `api` calls. We will do this in the following folder structure:

Apart from the folder structure created by React Native's CLI, we added the following folders and files:

- `src/components`: This will hold the reusable visual components.
- `src/reducers`: This will store the reducers, which modify the state of the app by detecting which actions were triggered.
- `src/screens`: This will store all the different visual containers connecting them to the app state through Redux.
- `src/api.js`: By the end of the chapter, we will have all the required API calls mocked inside this file. In case we wanted to connect to a real API, we would just need to change this file to make HTTP requests to the proper endpoints.
- `src/main.js`: This is the entry point to the app and will set up the navigation components and initialize the store in which the app's state will live.

The `src/components` folder will contain the following files:

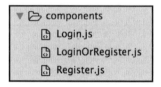

The `src/reducers` will hold the three different data domains in our app: user, payment, and products:

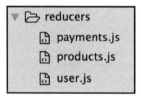

Last, the `screens` folder will store a file for each of the screens the user will be able to see in the app:

Let's take a look now at the `package.json` file we will use to install all required libraries for this app:

```
/*** package.json ***/

{
  "name": "ecommerce",
  "version": "0.0.1",
  "private": true,
  "scripts": {
    "start": "node node_modules/react-native/local-cli/cli.js start",
    "test": "jest",
    "ios": "react-native run-ios",
    "android": "react-native run-android"
  },
  "dependencies": {
    "native-base": "^2.3.1",
    "prop-types": "^15.5.10",
    "react": "16.0.0-alpha.12",
    "react-native": "0.48.3",
    "react-native-credit-card-input": "^0.3.3",
    "react-navigation": "^1.0.0-beta.11",
    "react-redux": "^5.0.6",
    "redux": "^3.7.2",
    "redux-thunk": "^2.2.0"
  },
  "devDependencies": {
    "babel-eslint": "^7.2.3",
    "babel-jest": "20.0.3",
    "babel-plugin-lodash": "^3.2.11",
    "babel-plugin-module-resolver": "^2.7.1",
    "babel-plugin-transform-builtin-extend": "^1.1.2",
    "babel-plugin-transform-react-jsx-source": "^6.22.0",
```

```
      "babel-plugin-transform-runtime": "^6.23.0",
      "babel-preset-env": "^1.6.0",
      "babel-preset-es2015": "^6.24.1",
      "babel-preset-react-native": "2.0.0",
      "babel-preset-stage-0": "^6.24.1",
      "eslint-config-airbnb": "^15.1.0",
      "eslint-config-prettier": "^2.3.0",
      "eslint-config-rallycoding": "^3.2.0",
      "eslint-import-resolver-babel-module": "^3.0.0",
      "eslint-import-resolver-webpack": "^0.8.3",
      "eslint-plugin-flowtype": "^2.35.0",
      "eslint-plugin-import": "^2.7.0",
      "eslint-plugin-jsx-a11y": "^5.1.1",
      "eslint-plugin-prettier": "^2.1.2",
      "eslint-plugin-react": "^7.2.0",
      "eslint-plugin-react-native": "^3.0.1",
      "jest": "20.0.4",
      "prettier": "^1.5.3",
      "prettier-package-json": "^1.4.0",
      "react-test-renderer": "16.0.0-alpha.12"
    },
    "jest": {
      "preset": "react-native"
    }
  }
```

We will be using the following extra libraries for our app:

- native-base: This is for styled components.
- prop-types: This is for property validation inside components.
- react-native-credit-card-input: This is for the user to enter her credit card details.
- react-redux: This and Redux are used for state management.
- redux-thunk: This is for connecting Redux to asynchronous calls.

Besides all these dependencies, we will add some other dev dependencies, which will help our developers write code in a very comfortable and confident way:

- babel-eslint: This is for linting our ES6 code.
- eslint-config-airbnb: This is the set of coding styles we will use.
- prettier: This is the code formatter we will use to support ES6 and JSX.

Having this `package.json` in place, we are ready to install all these dependencies by running:

```
npm install
```

Before starting to write code let's configure our linting rules and the text editor to take full advantage of the code formatting tools we will use in this chapter.

Linting and code formatting

Writing clean, bug-free code is challenging. There are a lot of pitfalls that we may face such as indentation, importing/exporting misses, tags not closed, and so on. Having to overcome all of them manually is a tough job which can distract us from our main purpose: writing functional code. Luckily, there are a handful of very useful tools to help us with this task.

The tools we will be using in this chapter to ensure our code is clean will be ESLint (`https://eslint.org/`) and Prettier (`https://github.com/prettier/prettier`).

ESLint will be in charge of identifying and reporting on patterns found in the ES6/JavaScript code, with the goal of making the code more consistent and avoiding bugs. For example, ESLint will flag any use of non-declared variables, exposing the error while we are writing code instead of waiting until compilation.

On the other hand, Prettier enforces a consistent code style across your entire codebase because it disregards the original styling by parsing it away and reprinting it with its own rules that take the maximum line length into account, wrapping code when necessary.

We can also use ESLint to enforce Prettier code styles directly in our browser. Our first step will be to configure ESLint to adapt to the formatting and linting rules we want to enforce in our project. In the case of this app, we will follow Airbnb's and Prettier's rules as we already installed them as a developer's dependency in this project.

To ensure ESLint will use these rules, we will create a `.eslintrc` file containing all the options we want to set up when linting:

```
/*** .eslintrc ***/

{
  "extends": ["airbnb", "prettier", "prettier/react", "prettier/flowtype"],
  "globals": {
    "queryTree": false
  },
  "plugins": ["react", "react-native", "flowtype", "prettier"],
```

```
"env": { "es6": true, "jest": true },
"parser": "babel-eslint",
"rules": {
  "prettier/prettier": [
    "error",
    {
      "trailingComma": "all",
      "singleQuote": true,
      "bracketSpacing": true,
      "tabWidth": 2
    }
  ],
  ...

}
```

We won't explore much in how to configure ESLint much in this book as their documentation is quite extensive and well explained. For this project, we will only need to extend Airbnb's and Prettier's rules while setting the corresponding plugins (`react`, `react-native`, `flowtype`, and `prettier`) in the configuration file.

Setting rules for the linter is a matter of taste, and in case of not having had much experience with it, it is always good to start with a set of prebuilt rules (such as the Airbnb rules) and modify them one rule at a time.

Finally, we would need to configure our code editor to display those rules, flag them, and ideally fix them on saving. Visual Studio Code does a very good job at integrating these linting/code formatting rules as its ESLint plugin (`https://github.com/Microsoft/vscode-eslint`) does all the work for us. It is highly recommended to enable the `eslint.autoFixOnSave` option to ensure the editor fixes all the code formatting issues after saving the file we are working on.

Now that we have our linting tools in place, let's start writing our app's codebase.

Indexes and main files

Both the iOS and Android platforms will share the same codebase using `src/main.js` as an entry point. Therefore, we will change `index.ios.js` and `index.android.js` to import `main.js` and initialize the app with that component as a root:

```
/*** index.ios.js and index.android.js ***/

import { AppRegistry } from 'react-native';
import App from './src/main';
```

```
AppRegistry.registerComponent('ecommerce', () => App);
```

This is the same structure we used for all apps sharing codebase throughout the book. Our `main.js` file should now initialize the navigation components and set up the store we will use to hold the app's state:

```javascript
/*** src/main.js ***/

import React from 'react';
import {
  DrawerNavigator,
  TabNavigator,
  StackNavigator,
} from 'react-navigation';
import { Platform } from 'react-native';

import { Provider } from 'react-redux';
import { createStore, combineReducers, applyMiddleware } from 'redux';
import thunk from 'redux-thunk';
import paymentsReducer from './reducers/payments';
import productsReducer from './reducers/products';
import userReducer from './reducers/user';

import ProductList from './screens/ProductList';
import ProductDetail from './screens/ProductDetail';
import MyCart from './screens/MyCart';
import MyProfile from './screens/MyProfile';
import Payment from './screens/Payment';
import PaymentConfirmation from './screens/PaymentConfirmation';
import Sales from './screens/Sales';

const ProductsNavigator = StackNavigator({
  ProductList: { screen: ProductList },
  ProductDetail: { screen: ProductDetail },
});

const PurchaseNavigator = StackNavigator({
  MyCart: { screen: MyCart },
  Payment: { screen: Payment },
  PaymentConfirmation: { screen: PaymentConfirmation },
});

let Navigator;
if (Platform.OS === 'ios') {
  Navigator = TabNavigator(
    {
      Home: { screen: ProductsNavigator },
      MyCart: { screen: PurchaseNavigator },
```

```
        MyProfile: { screen: MyProfile },
        Sales: { screen: Sales },
      },
      {
        tabBarOptions: {
          inactiveTintColor: '#aaa',
          activeTintColor: '#000',
          showLabel: true,
        },
      },
    );
  } else {
    Navigator = DrawerNavigator({
      Home: { screen: ProductsNavigator },
      MyCart: { screen: MyCart },
      MyProfile: { screen: MyProfile },
      Sales: { screen: Sales },
    });
  }

  const store = createStore(
    combineReducers({ paymentsReducer, productsReducer, userReducer }),
    applyMiddleware(thunk),
  );

  export default () => (
    <Provider store={store}>
      <Navigator />
    </Provider>
  );
```

Our main navigator (Navigator) will be a tabbed navigation on iOS and a drawer navigator on Android. This navigator will be the root for the app and will use two nested stacked navigators (ProductsNavigator and PurchaseNavigator), which will cover the following journeys:

- ProductsNavigator: **ProductList | ProductDetail**
- PurchaseNavigator: **MyCart | Payment | PaymentConfirmation**

Each step in each journey is a specific screen in the app.

 Login and registration are not steps in those journeys since they will be treated as pop-up screens displaying only if they are needed.

The last step in this file is in charge of setting up Redux, applying all the reducers and middleware (only `redux-thunk` in our case), which will be in place for this project:

```
const store = createStore(
  combineReducers({ paymentsReducer, productsReducer, userReducer }),
  applyMiddleware(thunk),
);
```

Once `store` is created, we pass it to the provider in the root of our app to make sure the state will be shared among all the screens. Before moving into each individual screen, let's create our reducers and actions so that we can have them available to be used when building the screens.

Reducers

In previous chapters, we split our Redux-specific code (reducers, actions, and action creators) in the standard way that is documented in Redux's documentation. To make it easy to maintain in the future, we will use a different approach for this app: Redux Ducks (`https://github.com/erikras/ducks-modular-redux`).

Redux Ducks is a proposal for bundling together reducers, action types, and actions when using Redux. Instead of creating separate folders for reducers and actions, they are put together in files based on which kind of functionality they handle, reducing the number of files to deal with when implementing new features.

Let's start with the `products` reducer:

```
/*** src/reducers/products.js ***/

import { get } from '../api';

// Actions
const FETCH = 'products/FETCH';
const FETCH_SUCCESS = 'products/FETCH_SUCCESS';
const FETCH_ERROR = 'products/FETCH_ERROR';
const ADD_TO_CART = 'products/ADD_TO_CART';
const REMOVE_FROM_CART = 'products/REMOVE_FROM_CART';
const RESET_CART = 'products/RESET_CART';

// Reducer
const initialState = {
  loading: false,
  cart: [],
  products: [],
```

```
  };
export default function reducer(state = initialState, action = {}) {
  let product;
  let i;
  switch (action.type) {
    case FETCH:
      return { ...state, loading: true };
    case FETCH_SUCCESS:
      return {
        ...state,
        products: action.payload.products,
        loading: false,
        error: null,
      };
    case FETCH_ERROR:
      return { ...state, error: action.payload.error, loading: false };
    case ADD_TO_CART:
      product = state.cart.find(p => p.id ===
                action.payload.product.id);
      if (product) {
        product.quantity += 1;
        return {
          ...state,
          cart: state.cart.slice(),
        };
      }
      product = action.payload.product;
      product.quantity = 1;
      return {
        ...state,
        cart: state.cart.slice().concat([action.payload.product]),
      };
    case REMOVE_FROM_CART:
      i = state.cart.findIndex(p => p.id ===
          action.payload.product.id);
      if (state.cart[i].quantity === 1) {
        state.cart.splice(i, 1);
      } else {
        state.cart[i].quantity -= 1;
      }
      return {
        ...state,
        cart: state.cart.slice(),
      };
    case RESET_CART:
      return {
        ...state,
        cart: [],
```

```
    };
  default:
    return state;
  }
}

// Action Creators
export function addProductToCart(product) {
  return { type: ADD_TO_CART, payload: { product } };
}

export function removeProductFromCart(product) {
  return { type: REMOVE_FROM_CART, payload: { product } };
}

export function fetchProducts() {
  return dispatch => {
    dispatch({ type: FETCH });
    get('/products')
      .then(products =>
        dispatch({ type: FETCH_SUCCESS, payload: { products } }),
      )
      .catch(error => dispatch({ type: FETCH_ERROR, payload: { error } }));
  };
}

export function resetCart() {
  return { type: RESET_CART };
}
```

This file handles all the business logic related to products in our app. Let's review each action creator and how it modifies the state when processed by the reducer:

- addProductToCart(): This will dispatch the ADD_TO_CART action, which will be picked up by the reducer. If the provided product is already present in the cart inside the state, it will increase the quantity by one item. Otherwise, it will insert the product into the cart and set its quantity to one.
- removeProductFromCart(): This action does the opposite to the previous one. It decreases the quantity of this product if already present in the cart stored in the state. If the quantity of this product is one, the reducer will remove the product from the cart.

- `fetchProducts()`: This is an asynchronous action and therefore will return a function for `redux-thunk` to pick it up. It will make a GET request (implemented by the `get()` function in the `api.json` file) to the API to the `/products` endpoint. It will also handle the response from this endpoint, dispatching a `FETCH_SUCCESS` action when the request is successfully fulfilled, or a `FETCH_ERROR` action in case the request is errored out.
- `resetCart()`: This dispatches a `RESET_CART` action, which will be used by the reducer to clear all the cart details from the state.

As we are following Redux Ducks recommendation, all these actions are put together in the same file making it easy to determine what actions do and what effect they cause in the application state.

Let's move now to the next reducer: the `user` reducer:

```
/*** src/reducers/user.js ***/

import { post } from '../api';

// Actions
const LOGIN = 'user/LOGIN';
const LOGIN_SUCCESS = 'user/LOGIN_SUCCESS';
const LOGIN_ERROR = 'user/LOGIN_ERROR';
const REGISTER = 'user/REGISTER';
const REGISTER_SUCCESS = 'user/REGISTER_SUCCESS';
const REGISTER_ERROR = 'user/REGISTER_ERROR';
const LOGOUT = 'user/LOGOUT';

// Reducer
export default function reducer(state = {}, action = {}) {
  switch (action.type) {
    case LOGIN:
    case REGISTER:
      return { ...state, user: null, loading: true, error: null };
    case LOGIN_SUCCESS:
    case REGISTER_SUCCESS:
      return {
        ...state,
        user: action.payload.user,
        loading: false,
        error: null,
      };
    case LOGIN_ERROR:
    case REGISTER_ERROR:
      return {
        ...state,
```

```
          user: null,
          loading: false,
          error: action.payload.error,
        };
      case LOGOUT:
        return {
          ...state,
          user: null,
        };
      default:
        return state;
    }
}

// Action Creators
export function login({ email, password }) {
  return dispatch => {
    dispatch({ type: LOGIN });
    post('/login', { email, password })
      .then(user => dispatch({ type: LOGIN_SUCCESS,
      payload: { user } }))
      .catch(error => dispatch({ type: LOGIN_ERROR,
      payload: { error } }));
  };
}

export function register({
  email,
  repeatEmail,
  name,
  password,
  address,
  postcode,
  city,
}) {
  if (
    !email ||
    !repeatEmail ||
    !name ||
    !password ||
    !name ||
    !address ||
    !postcode ||
    !city
  ) {
    return {
      type: REGISTER_ERROR,
      payload: { error: 'All fields are mandatory' },
```

```
      };
    }
    if (email !== repeatEmail) {
      return {
        type: REGISTER_ERROR,
        payload: { error: "Email fields don't match" },
      };
    }
    return dispatch => {
      dispatch({ type: REGISTER });
      post('/register', {
        email,
        name,
        password,
        address,
        postcode,
        city,
      })
        .then(user => dispatch({ type: REGISTER_SUCCESS, payload:
                     { user } }))
        .catch(error => dispatch({ type: REGISTER_ERROR, payload:
                     { error } }));
    };
  }

  export function logout() {
    return { type: LOGOUT };
  }
```

The action creators in this reducer are quite straightforward:

- `login()`: This takes an `email` and `password` to dispatch the `LOGIN` action and then makes a `POST` request to the `/login` endpoint to validate the credentials. If the API call becomes successful, the action creator will dispatch a `LOGIN_SUCCESS` action logging the user in. In case the request fails, it will dispatch a `LOGIN_ERROR` action so the user can know what happened.
- `register()`: This is similar to the `login()` action creator; it will dispatch a `REGISTER` action, then a `REGISTER_SUCCESS` or `REGISTER_ERROR`, depending on how the API call returns. If the registration was successful, the user data will be stored in the application's state, flagging that the user has logged in.
- `logout()`: This dispatches a `LOGOUT` action, which will make the reducer clear the `user` object in the application state.

The last reducer deals with payments data:

```
/*** src/reducers/payments.js ***/

import { post } from '../api';

// Actions
const PAY = 'products/PAY';
const PAY_SUCCESS = 'products/PAY_SUCCESS';
const PAY_ERROR = 'products/PAY_ERROR';
const RESET_PAYMENT = 'products/RESET_PAYMENT';

// Reducer
export default function reducer(state = {}, action = {}) {
  switch (action.type) {
    case PAY:
      return { ...state, loading: true, paymentConfirmed: false,
               error: null };
    case PAY_SUCCESS:
      return {
        ...state,
        paymentConfirmed: true,
        loading: false,
        error: null,
      };
    case PAY_ERROR:
      return {
        ...state,
        loading: false,
        paymentConfirmed: false,
        error: action.payload.error,
      };
    case RESET_PAYMENT:
      return { loading: false, paymentConfirmed: false, error: null };
    default:
      return state;
  }
}

// Action Creators
export function pay(user, cart, card) {
  return dispatch => {
    dispatch({ type: PAY });
    post('/pay', { user, cart, card })
      .then(() => dispatch({ type: PAY_SUCCESS }))
      .catch(error => dispatch({ type: PAY_ERROR,
              payload: { error } }));
  };
```

```
}

export function resetPayment() {
  return { type: RESET_PAYMENT };
}
```

There are only two action creators in this reducer:

- pay(): This takes a user, a cart, and a credit card and calls the /pay endpoint in the API to make a payment. If the payment is successful, it triggers a PAY_SUCCESS action, otherwise, it triggers a PAY_ERROR action to notify the user.
- resetPayment(): This clears any payment data by triggering the RESET_PAYMENT action.

We have seen these action creators contact the API in several ways. Let's now create some API methods, so the action creators can interact with the application's backend.

API

The API service we will be using will use two HTTP methods (GET and POST) and four endpoints (/products, /login, /register, and /pay). We will mock up this service for testing and development reasons but will leave the implementation open to plug in external endpoints easily at a later stage:

```
/*** src/api.js ***/

export const get = uri =>
  new Promise(resolve => {
    let response;

    switch (uri) {
      case '/products':
        response = [
          {
            id: 1,
            name: 'Mastering Docker - Second Edition',
            author: 'James Cameron',
            img:
              'https://d1ldz4te4covpm.cloudfront.net/sites/default
              /files/imagecache/ppv4_main_book_cover
              /B06565_MockupCover_0.png',
            price: 39.58,
          },
```

```
        ...

      ];
      break;
    default:
      return null;
    }

    setTimeout(() => resolve(response), 1000);
    return null;
  });

export const post = (uri, data) =>
  new Promise((resolve, reject) => {
    let response;

    switch (uri) {
      case '/login':
        if (data.email === 'test@test.com' && data.password === 'test')
        {
          response = {
            email: 'test@test.com',
            name: 'Test Testson',
            address: '123 test street',
            postcode: '2761XZ',
            city: 'Testington',
          };
        } else {
          setTimeout(() => reject('Unauthorised'), 1000);
          return null;
        }
        break;
      case '/pay':
        if (data.card.cvc === '123') {
          response = true;
        } else {
          setTimeout(() => reject('Payment not authorised'), 1000);
          return null;
        }
        break;
      case '/register':
        response = data;
        break;
      default:
        return null;
    }

    setTimeout(() => resolve(response), 1000);
```

```
        return null;
    });

    export const put = () => {};
```

All calls are wrapped inside a `setTimeout()` function with 1-second delays to simulate network activity so indicators can be tested. The service only replies successfully when credentials are `test@test.com/test`. On the other hand, the `pay()` service only returns a successful response when the **CVC/CVV** code is `123`. The register call just returns the provided data as successfully registered user data.

 This setTimeout() trick is used to mock asynchronous calls up as they would happen with a real backend. It is an useful way to develop front-end solutions before the backend or testing environments are ready.

Let's now move on to the screens in the application.

ProductList

Our home screen displays a list of products available to be purchased:

```
/*** src/screens/ProductList.js ***/

import React from 'react';
import { ScrollView, TouchableOpacity } from 'react-native';
import PropTypes from 'prop-types';

import { bindActionCreators } from 'redux';
import { connect } from 'react-redux';
import {
  Spinner,
  Icon,
  List,
  ListItem,
  Thumbnail,
  Body,
  Text,
} from 'native-base';
import * as ProductActions from '../reducers/products';

class ProductList extends React.Component {
  static navigationOptions = {
    drawerLabel: 'Home',
    tabBarIcon: () => <Icon name="home" />,
```

```
    };

    componentWillMount() {
      this.props.fetchProducts();
    }

    onProductPress(product) {
      this.props.navigation.navigate('ProductDetail', { product });
    }

    render() {
      return (
        <ScrollView>
          {this.props.loading && <Spinner />}
          <List>
            {this.props.products.map(p => (
              <ListItem key={p.id}>
                <Thumbnail square height={80} source={{ uri: p.img }} />
                <Body>
                  <TouchableOpacity onPress={() =>
                   this.onProductPress(p)}>
                    <Text>{p.name}</Text>
                    <Text note>${p.price}</Text>
                  </TouchableOpacity>
                </Body>
              </ListItem>
            ))}
          </List>
        </ScrollView>
      );
    }
}

ProductList.propTypes = {
  fetchProducts: PropTypes.func.isRequired,
  products: PropTypes.array.isRequired,
  loading: PropTypes.bool.isRequired,
  navigation: PropTypes.any.isRequired,
};

function mapStateToProps(state) {
  return {
    products: state.productsReducer.products || [],
    loading: state.productsReducer.loading,
  };
}

function mapStateActionsToProps(dispatch) {
```

```
    return bindActionCreators(ProductActions, dispatch);
}

export default connect(mapStateToProps,
mapStateActionsToProps)(ProductList);
```

Right after this screen is mounted, it will retrieve the latest list of available products by invoking `this.props.fetchProducts();`. This will trigger a re-render in the screen, so all the available books are displayed on the screen. For that to happen, we rely on Redux updating the state (through the product reducer) and injecting the new state into this screen by calling the `connect` method, to which we will need to pass `mapStateToProps` and `mapStateActionsToProps` functions.

`mapStateToProps` will be in charge of extracting the list of products from `state` while `mapStateActionsToProps` will connect each action with the `dispatch()` function, which will connect those actions with the Redux state, applying each triggered action to all the reducers. In this screen, we are only interested in product-related actions, so we will bind only `ProductActions` and the `dispatch` function together through the `bindActionCreators` Redux function.

Inside the `render` method, we use the `map` function to translate the list of retrieved products into several `<ListItem/>` components, which will be displayed inside `<List/>`. Above this list, we will display `<Spinner/>` while waiting for the network request to be fulfilled: `{this.props.loading && <Spinner />}`.

We also added property validation through the `prop-types` library:

```
ProductList.propTypes = {
  fetchProducts: PropTypes.func.isRequired,
  products: PropTypes.array.isRequired,
  loading: PropTypes.bool.isRequired,
  navigation: PropTypes.any.isRequired,
};
```

This means we will get a warning every time this component receives a wrongly typed prop, or it actually fails to receive one of the required props. In this case, we expect to receive:

- A function named `fetchProducts`, which will request the list of available products to the API. It will be provided by Redux through `mapStateActionsToProps` as defined on this screen.
- A `products` array that contains the list of available products. This will be injected by Redux through the previously stated `mapStateToProps` function.

- A loading Boolean to flag network activity (also provided by Redux through `mapStateToProps`).
- A navigation object provided by `react-navigation` automatically. We mark it as type `any` as it is an external object, which may change its type out of our control.

All these will be available to be used inside our component's props (`this.props`).

The last thing to note about this container is how we are going to deal with the user actions. In this screen, there is only one action: the user clicking on a product item to see its details:

```
onProductPress(product) {
    this.props.navigation.navigate('ProductDetail', { product });
}
```

When the user taps on a specific product, this screen will call the `navigate` function in the `navigation` prop to move to our next screen, `ProductDetail`. Instead of saving the selected product in the state through an action, we will pass it directly using `navigation` options to simplify our store.

ProductDetail

This screen will show the user all the details about the selected product and allow her to add this selected product to her cart:

```
/*** src/screens/ProductDetail.js ***/

import React from 'react';
import { Image, ScrollView } from 'react-native';

import { bindActionCreators } from 'redux';
import { connect } from 'react-redux';
import PropTypes from 'prop-types';
import { Icon, Button, Text } from 'native-base';
import * as ProductsActions from '../reducers/products';

class ProductDetail extends React.Component {
  static navigationOptions = {
    drawerLabel: 'Home',
    tabBarIcon: () => <Icon name="home" />,
  };

  onBuyPress(product) {
    this.props.addProductToCart(product);
```

```
        this.props.navigation.goBack();
        setTimeout((() => this.props.navigation.navigate('MyCart',
                        { product }), 0);
    }

    render() {
      const { navigation } = this.props;
      const { state } = navigation;
      const { params } = state;
      const { product } = params;
      return (
        <ScrollView>
          <Image
            style={{
              height: 200,
              width: 160,
              alignSelf: 'center',
              marginTop: 20,
            }}
            source={{ uri: product.img }}
          />
          <Text
            style={{
              alignSelf: 'center',
              marginTop: 20,
              fontSize: 30,
              fontWeight: 'bold',
            }}
          >
            ${product.price}
          </Text>
          <Text
            style={{
              alignSelf: 'center',
              margin: 20,
            }}
          >
            Lorem ipsum dolor sit amet, consectetur
            adipiscing elit. Nullam nec
            eros quis magna vehicula blandit at nec velit.
            Mauris porta risus non
            lectus ultricies lacinia. Phasellus molestie metus ac
            metus dapibus,
            nec maximus arcu interdum. In hac habitasse platea dictumst.
            Suspendisse fermentum iaculis ex, faucibus semper turpis
            vestibulum quis.
          </Text>
          <Button
```

```
          block
          style={{ margin: 20 }}
          onPress={() => this.onBuyPress(product)}
        >
          <Text>Buy!</Text>
        </Button>
      </ScrollView>
    );
  }
}


ProductDetail.propTypes = {
  navigation: PropTypes.any.isRequired,
  addProductToCart: PropTypes.func.isRequired,
};

ProductDetail.navigationOptions = props => {
  const { navigation } = props;
  const { state } = navigation;
  const { params } = state;
  return {
    tabBarIcon: () => <Icon name="home" />,
    headerTitle: params.product.name,
  };
};

function mapStateToProps(state) {
  return {
    user: state.userReducer.user,
  };
}
function mapStateActionsToProps(dispatch) {
  return bindActionCreators(ProductsActions, dispatch);
}

export default connect(mapStateToProps,
mapStateActionsToProps)(ProductDetail);
```

ProductDetail requires Redux to provide it with the user details stored in state. This is achieved by calling the connect method, passing a mapStateToProps function which will extract the user from the specified state and return it to be injected as prop in the screen. It also requires an action from Redux: addProductToCart. This action just stores the selected product in the store when the user expressee her wish to buy it.

The render() method in this screen shows <ScrollView /> wrapping the book image, price, description (we will display a fake lorem ipsum description for now), and a Buy! button, which will be connected to the addProductToCart action provided by Redux:

```
onBuyPress(product) {
    this.props.addProductToCart(product);
    this.props.navigation.goBack();
    setTimeout(() => this.props.navigation.navigate('MyCart',
                     { product }), 0);
}
```

The onBuyPress() method invokes the mentioned action and does a small navigation trick afterwards. It goes back by calling the goBack() method on the navigation object to remove the ProductDetail screen from the navigation stack, as the user won't need it anymore after adding the product to the cart. Immediately after doing this, the onBuyPress() method will invoke the navigate method on the navigation object to be moved and display the state of the user's cart in the MyCart screen. We are using setTimeout here to make sure we wait until the previous call (this.props.navigation.goBack();) has finished all the navigation tasks and the object is again ready for us to use. Waiting for 0 seconds should be enough, since we just want to wait for the call stack to be cleared.

Let's take a look at what the MyCart screen looks like now.

MyCart

This screen expects Redux to inject the cart stored in the state, so it can render all the items in the cart for the user to review before confirming the purchase:

```
/*** src/screens/MyCart.js ***/

import React from 'react';
import { ScrollView, View } from 'react-native';

import { bindActionCreators } from 'redux';
import { connect } from 'react-redux';
import PropTypes from 'prop-types';
import {
  ListItem,
  Text,
  Icon,
  Button,
  Badge,
```

```
  Header,
  Title,
} from 'native-base';

import * as ProductActions from '../reducers/products';

class MyCart extends React.Component {
  static navigationOptions = {
    drawerLabel: 'My Cart',
    tabBarIcon: () => <Icon name="cart" />,
  };

  onTrashPress(product) {
    this.props.removeProductFromCart(product);
  }

  render() {
    return (
      <View>
        <ScrollView>
          {this.props.cart.map((p, i) => (
            <ListItem key={i} style={{ justifyContent:
                            'space-between' }}>
              <Badge primary>
                <Text>{p.quantity}</Text>
              </Badge>
              <Text> {p.name}</Text>
              <Button
                icon
                danger
                small
                transparent
                onPress={() => this.onTrashPress(p)}
              >
                <Icon name="trash" />
              </Button>
            </ListItem>
          ))}
          {this.props.cart.length > 0 && (
            <View>
              <Text style={{ alignSelf: 'flex-end', margin: 10 }}>
                Total: ${this.props.cart.reduce(
                  (sum, p) => sum + p.price * p.quantity,
                  0,
                )}
              </Text>
              <View style={{ flexDirection: 'row',
                justifyContent: 'center' }}>
```

```
                        <Button
                          style={{ margin: 10 }}
                          onPress={() =>
                          this.props.navigation.navigate('Home')}
                        >
                          <Text>Keep buying</Text>
                        </Button>
                        <Button
                          style={{ margin: 10 }}
                          onPress={() =>
                          this.props.navigation.navigate('Payment')}
                        >
                          <Text>Confirm purchase</Text>
                        </Button>
                    </View>
                  </View>
              )}
              {this.props.cart.length == 0 && (
                <Text style={{ alignSelf: 'center', margin: 30 }}>
                  There are no products in the cart
                </Text>
              )}
          </ScrollView>
        </View>
    );
  }
}

MyCart.propTypes = {
  cart: PropTypes.array.isRequired,
  navigation: PropTypes.object.isRequired,
  removeProductFromCart: PropTypes.func.isRequired,
};

function mapStateToProps(state) {
  return {
    user: state.userReducer.user,
    cart: state.productsReducer.cart || [],
    loading: state.userReducer.loading,
    error: state.userReducer.error,
    paying: state.paymentsReducer.loading,
  };
}
function mapStateActionsToProps(dispatch) {
  return bindActionCreators(ProductActions, dispatch);
}

export default connect(mapStateToProps, mapStateActionsToProps)(MyCart);
```

Apart from the cart itself, as we can see in the `propTypes` definition, this screen needs the action `removeProductFromCart` from `ProductActions`, and the `navigation` object to be provided to navigate to the `Payment` screen when the user is ready to confirm her purchase.

In summary, the user can take three actions from here:

- Removing an item from the cart by clicking on the **Trash** icon on each product row (invoking `this.onTrashPress()`)
- Navigating to the `Payment` screen to complete her purchase (invoking `this.props.navigation.navigate('Payment')`)
- Navigating to the home screen to keep buying products (invoking `this.props.navigation.navigate('Home')`)

Let's continue to the purchase journey by reviewing the `Payment` screen.

Payment

We will use the `react-native-credit-card-input` library to capture the user's credit card details. For this screen to work, we will request the cart, the user, and several important actions from Redux:

```
/*** src/screens/Payment.js ***/

import React from 'react';
import { View } from 'react-native';

import { CreditCardInput } from 'react-native-credit-card-input';
import { bindActionCreators } from 'redux';
import { connect } from 'react-redux';
import { Icon, Button, Text, Spinner, Title } from 'native-base';
import PropTypes from 'prop-types';
import * as PaymentsActions from '../reducers/payments';
import * as UserActions from '../reducers/user';
import LoginOrRegister from '../components/LoginOrRegister';

class Payment extends React.Component {
  static navigationOptions = {
    drawerLabel: 'MyCart',
    tabBarIcon: () => <Icon name="cart" />,
  };
  state = {
    validCardDetails: false,
    cardDetails: null,
```

```
  };
  onCardInputChange(creditCardForm) {
    this.setState({
      validCardDetails: creditCardForm.valid,
      cardDetails: creditCardForm.values,
    });
  }

  componentWillReceiveProps(newProps) {
    if (this.props.paying && newProps.paymentConfirmed) {
      this.props.navigation.navigate('PaymentConfirmation');
    }
  }

  render() {
    return (
      <View
        style={{
          flex: 1,
          alignSelf: 'stretch',
          paddingTop: 10,
        }}
      >
        {this.props.cart.length > 0 &&
        !this.props.user && (
          <LoginOrRegister
            login={this.props.login}
            register={this.props.register}
            logout={this.props.logout}
            loading={this.props.loading}
            error={this.props.error}
          />
        )}
        {this.props.cart.length > 0 &&
        this.props.user && (
          <View>
            <Title style={{ margin: 10 }}>
              Paying: $
              {this.props.cart.reduce(
                (sum, p) => sum + p.price * p.quantity,
                0,
              )}
            </Title>
            <CreditCardInput onChange=
            {this.onCardInputChange.bind(this)} />
            <Button
              block
              style={{ margin: 20 }}
```

```
                    onPress={() =>
                      this.props.pay(
                        this.props.user,
                        this.props.cart,
                        this.state.cardDetails,
                      )}
                    disabled={!this.state.validCardDetails}
                  >
                    <Text>Pay now</Text>
                  </Button>
                  {this.props.paying && <Spinner />}
                </View>
              )}
              {this.props.cart.length > 0 &&
              this.props.error && (
                <Text
                  style={{
                    alignSelf: 'center',
                    color: 'red',
                    position: 'absolute',
                    bottom: 10,
                  }}
                >
                  {this.props.error}
                </Text>
              )}
              {this.props.cart.length === 0 && (
                <Text style={{ alignSelf: 'center', margin: 30 }}>
                  There are no products in the cart
                </Text>
              )}
          </View>
        );
      }
    }

Payment.propTypes = {
  user: PropTypes.object,
  cart: PropTypes.array,
  login: PropTypes.func.isRequired,
  register: PropTypes.func.isRequired,
  logout: PropTypes.func.isRequired,
  pay: PropTypes.func.isRequired,
  loading: PropTypes.bool,
  paying: PropTypes.bool,
  error: PropTypes.string,
  paymentConfirmed: PropTypes.bool,
  navigation: PropTypes.object.isRequired,
```

```
};

function mapStateToProps(state) {
  return {
    user: state.userReducer.user,
    cart: state.productsReducer.cart,
    loading: state.userReducer.loading,
    paying: state.paymentsReducer.loading,
    paymentConfirmed: state.paymentsReducer.paymentConfirmed,
    error: state.paymentsReducer.error || state.userReducer.error,
  };
}
function mapStateActionsToProps(dispatch) {
  return bindActionCreators(
    Object.assign({}, PaymentsActions, UserActions),
    dispatch,
  );
}

export default connect(mapStateToProps, mapStateActionsToProps)(Payment);
```

This is a complex component. Let's take a look at the props validation to understand its signature:

```
Payment.propTypes = {
  user: PropTypes.object,
  cart: PropTypes.array,
  login: PropTypes.func.isRequired,
  register: PropTypes.func.isRequired,
  logout: PropTypes.func.isRequired,
  pay: PropTypes.func.isRequired,
  loading: PropTypes.bool,
  paying: PropTypes.bool,
  error: PropTypes.string,
  paymentConfirmed: PropTypes.bool,
  navigation: PropTypes.object.isRequired,
};
```

The following props need to be passed for the component to work properly:

- `user`: We need the user to check if she is logged in. In case she is not, we will display the login/registration components instead of the credit card input.
- `cart`: We need it to calculate and display the total to be charged to the credit card.
- `login`: This action will be invoked if the user decides to log in from this screen.

- register: This action will be invoked if the user decides to register from this screen.
- logout: This action is needed for the <LoginOrRegister /> component to work, so it needs to be provided from Redux so it can be injected into the child <LoginOrRegister /> component.
- pay: This action will be triggered when the user has entered valid credit card details and pressed the **Pay now** button.
- loading: This is a flag for the child <LoginOrRegister /> component to work properly.
- paying: This flag will be used to display a spinner while the payment is being confirmed.
- error: This is a description of the last error to have happened when trying to pay or log in/register.
- paymentConfirmed: This flag will let the component know when/if the payment has gone through correctly.
- navigation: The navigation object used to navigate to other screens.

This component also has its own state:

```
state = {
    validCardDetails: false,
    cardDetails: null,
};
```

Both attributes in this state will be provided by <CreditCardInput /> (the main component form react-native-credit-card-input) and will hold the user's credit card details and their validity together.

To detect when the payment has been confirmed, we will use the React method componentWillReceiveProps:

```
componentWillReceiveProps(newProps) {
    if (this.props.paying && newProps.paymentConfirmed) {
      this.props.navigation.navigate('PaymentConfirmation');
    }
}
```

This method just detects when the prop paymentConfirmed changes from false to true in order to navigate to the PaymentConfirmation screen.

PaymentConfirmation

A simple screen displays a summary of the purchase just confirmed:

```
/*** src/screens/PaymentConfirmation ***/

import React from 'react';
import { View } from 'react-native';
import PropTypes from 'prop-types';

import { bindActionCreators } from 'redux';
import { connect } from 'react-redux';
import { NavigationActions } from 'react-navigation';
import { Icon, Title, Text, ListItem, Badge, Button } from 'native-base';

import * as UserActions from '../reducers/user';
import * as ProductActions from '../reducers/products';
import * as PaymentsActions from '../reducers/payments';

class PaymentConfirmation extends React.Component {
  static navigationOptions = {
    drawerLabel: 'MyCart',
    tabBarIcon: () => <Icon name="cart" />,
  };

  componentWillMount() {
    this.setState({ cart: this.props.cart }, () => {
      this.props.resetCart();
      this.props.resetPayment();
    });
  }

  continueShopping() {
    const resetAction = NavigationActions.reset({
      index: 0,
      actions: [NavigationActions.navigate({ routeName: 'MyCart' })],
    });
    this.props.navigation.dispatch(resetAction);
  }

  render() {
    return (
      <View>
        <Title style={{ marginTop: 20 }}>Your purchase is complete!
        </Title>
        <Text style={{ margin: 20 }}>
          Thank you for buying with us. We sent you an email with the
          confirmation details and an invoice.
```

```
          Here you can find a summary of
          your purchase:{' '}
        </Text>
        {this.state.cart.map((p, i) => (
          <ListItem key={i} style={{ justifyContent:
          'space-between' }}>
            <Badge primary>
              <Text>{p.quantity}</Text>
            </Badge>
            <Text> {p.name}</Text>
            <Text> {p.price * p.quantity}</Text>
          </ListItem>
        ))}
        <Text style={{ alignSelf: 'flex-end', margin: 10 }}>
          Total: ${this.state.cart.reduce(
            (sum, p) => sum + p.price * p.quantity,
            0,
          )}
        </Text>
        <Button
          block
          style={{ margin: 20 }}
          onPress={this.continueShopping.bind(this)}
        >
          <Text>Continue Shopping</Text>
        </Button>
      </View>
    );
  }
}

PaymentConfirmation.propTypes = {
  cart: PropTypes.array.isRequired,
  resetCart: PropTypes.func.isRequired,
  resetPayment: PropTypes.func.isRequired,
};

function mapStateToProps(state) {
  return {
    cart: state.productsReducer.cart || [],
  };
}
function mapStateActionsToProps(dispatch) {
  return bindActionCreators(
    Object.assign({}, PaymentsActions, ProductActions, UserActions),
    dispatch,
  );
}
```

```
export default connect(mapStateToProps, mapStateActionsToProps)(
  PaymentConfirmation,
);
```

The first thing this screen does is to save the app's state related to the cart in the own component's state:

```
componentWillMount() {
    this.setState({ cart: this.props.cart }, () => {
      this.props.resetCart();
      this.props.resetPayment();
    });
}
```

This is necessary because we want to reset the cart and payment details right after this screen is shown as it won't be needed on any further occasion. This is done by invoking both the resetCart() and resetPayment() actions provided by Redux.

The render method just maps the items in the cart (now saved in the component's state) into a list of views so the user can review her order. At the bottom of these views, we will display a button labeled **Continue Shopping**, which will return the user to the ProductList screen by calling the continueShopping method. Besides navigating to the ProductList screen, we need to reset the navigation so the purchase journey can be started from scratch the next time the user wants to buy some items. This is achieved by creating a reset navigation action and invoking this.props.navigation.dispatch(resetAction);.

 The method continueShopping calls NavigationActions.reset to clear the navigation stack and go back to the home screen. This method is usually called at the end of a user journey.

This screen completes the purchase journey, so let's focus now in a different part of the application: the user profile.

MyProfile

As we saw before, only logged-in users can complete purchases so we need a way for the users to log in, log out, register, and review their account details. This will be achieved by the `MyProfile` screen and the `<LonginOrRegister />` component:

```
/*** src/screens/MyProfile.js ***/

import React from 'react';
import { View, Button as LinkButton } from 'react-native';
import PropTypes from 'prop-types';

import { bindActionCreators } from 'redux';
import { connect } from 'react-redux';
import {
  Icon,
  Header,
  Title,
  Label,
  Input,
  Item,
  Form,
  Content,
} from 'native-base';

import * as UserActions from '../reducers/user';
import LoginOrRegister from '../components/LoginOrRegister';

class MyProfile extends React.Component {
  static navigationOptions = {
    drawerLabel: 'My Profile',
    tabBarIcon: () => <Icon name="person" />,
  };

  render() {
    return (
      <View
        style={{
          flex: 1,
          alignSelf: 'stretch',
        }}
      >
        <Header>
          <Title style={{ paddingTop: 10 }}>My Profile</Title>
        </Header>
        {!this.props.user && (
          <LoginOrRegister
```

```
          login={this.props.login}
          register={this.props.register}
          logout={this.props.logout}
          loading={this.props.loading}
          error={this.props.error}
        />
      )}
      {this.props.user && (
        <Content>
          <Form>
            <Item>
              <Item fixedLabel>
                <Label>Name</Label>
                <Input disabled placeholder={this.props.user.name} />
              </Item>
            </Item>
            <Item disabled>
              <Item fixedLabel>
                <Label>Email</Label>
                <Input disabled placeholder={this.props.user.email}
                />
              </Item>
            </Item>
            <Item disabled>
              <Item fixedLabel>
                <Label>Address</Label>
                <Input disabled placeholder={this.props.user.address}
                />
              </Item>
            </Item>
            <Item disabled>
              <Item fixedLabel&gt;
                <Label>Postcode</Label>
                <Input disabled placeholder=
                  {this.props.user.postcode} />
              </Item>
            </Item>
            <Item disabled>
              <Item fixedLabel>
                <Label>City</Label>
                <Input disabled placeholder={this.props.user.city} />
              </Item>
            </Item>
          </Form>
          <LinkButton title={'Logout'} onPress={() =>
            this.props.logout()} />
        </Content>
      )}
```

```
        </View>
      );
    }
  }

MyProfile.propTypes = {
  user: PropTypes.any,
  login: PropTypes.func.isRequired,
  register: PropTypes.func.isRequired,
  logout: PropTypes.func.isRequired,
  loading: PropTypes.bool,
  error: PropTypes.string,
};

function mapStateToProps(state) {
  return {
    user: state.userReducer.user || null,
    loading: state.userReducer.loading,
    error: state.userReducer.error,
  };
}
function mapStateActionsToProps(dispatch) {
  return bindActionCreators(UserActions, dispatch);
}

export default connect(mapStateToProps, mapStateActionsToProps)(MyProfile);
```

This screen receives the user from the app's state and a number of actions (login,
register, and logout), which will be fed into the <LoginOrRegister /> component to
enable login and registration. Most of the logic, therefore, will be deferred to
the <LoginOrRegister /> component, leaving the MyProfile screen with the tasks of
listing the user's account details and displaying a button for logging her out.

Let's review what the <LoginOrRegister /> component does and how.

LoginOrRegister

Actually, this component is compounded by two sub-components: <Login /> and
<Register />. The only task of <LoginOrRegister /> is to save the state of which
component (<Login /> or <Register />) should be displayed, showing it accordingly.

```
/*** src/components/LoginOrRegister.js ***/

import React from 'react';
import { View } from 'react-native';
```

```
import PropTypes from 'prop-types';

import Login from './Login';
import Register from './Register';

export default class LoginOrRegister extends React.Component {
  state = {
    display: 'login',
  };

  render() {
    return (
      <View
        style={{
          flex: 1,
          justifyContent: 'center',
          alignSelf: 'stretch',
        }}
      >
        {this.state.display === 'login' && (
          <Login
            login={this.props.login}
            changeToRegister={() => this.setState({ display:
            'register' })}
            loading={this.props.loading}
            error={this.props.error}
          />
        )}
        {this.state.display === 'register' && (
          <Register
            register={this.props.register}
            changeToLogin={() => this.setState({ display: 'login' })}
            loading={this.props.loading}
            error={this.props.error}
          />
        )}
      </View>
    );
  }
}

LoginOrRegister.propTypes = {
  error: PropTypes.string,
  login: PropTypes.func.isRequired,
  register: PropTypes.func.isRequired,
  loading: PropTypes.bool,
};
```

The state in this component can be changed by their child components as it passes a function to do so to each child:

```
changeToRegister={() => this.setState({ display: 'register' })}

...

changeToLogin={() => this.setState({ display: 'login' })}
```

Let's now take a look at how the <Login /> and <Register /> components will use these props to update their parents' state, switching from one view to another.

Login

The login view will be displayed by default on the parent component. Its task is to capture login information and call the login action once the user pushes the Login button:

```
/*** src/components/Login.js ***/

import React from 'react';
import { View, Button as LinkButton } from 'react-native';
import { Form, Item, Input, Content, Button, Text, Spinner } from 'native-base';
import PropTypes from 'prop-types';

class Login extends React.Component {
  state = { email: null, password: null };

  render() {
    return (
      <View style={{ flex: 1 }}>
        <Content>
          <Form>
            <Item>
              <Input
                placeholder="e-mail"
                keyboardType={'email-address'}
                autoCapitalize={'none'}
                onChangeText={email => this.setState({ email })}
              />
            </Item>
            <Item last>
              <Input
                placeholder="password"
                secureTextEntry
                onChangeText={password => this.setState({ password })}
```

```
                      />
                    </Item>
                    <Button
                      block
                      disabled={this.props.loading}
                      style={{ margin: 20 }}
                      onPress={() =>
                        this.props.login({
                          email: this.state.email,
                          password: this.state.password,
                        })}
                    >
                      <Text>Login</Text>
                    </Button>
                  </Form>

                  <LinkButton
                    title={'or Register'}
                    onPress={() => this.props.changeToRegister()}
                  />
                  {this.props.loading && <Spinner />}
                </Content>
                {this.props.error && (
                  <Text
                    style={{
                      alignSelf: 'center',
                      color: 'red',
                      position: 'absolute',
                      bottom: 10,
                    }}
                  >
                    {this.props.error}
                  </Text>
                )}
              </View>
            );
          }
        }

Login.propTypes = {
  error: PropTypes.string,
  loading: PropTypes.bool,
  login: PropTypes.func.isRequired,
  changeToRegister: PropTypes.func.isRequired,
};

export default Login;
```

Two inputs capture the email and the password and save them into the component state as the inputs are being changed. Once the user has finished entering her credentials, she will press the `Login` button and trigger the login action passing the email and password from the component's state.

There is also a `<LinkButton />` labeled `or Register`, which will invoke (when pressed) the `this.props.changeToRegister()` function passed by its parent, `<LoginOrRegister />`.

Register

Similarly to the login form, the `<Register />` component is a list of input fields saving its changes into the component state until the user is confident enough to press the `Register` button:

```
import React from 'react';
import { View, Button as LinkButton } from 'react-native';
import { Form, Item, Input, Content, Button, Text, Spinner } from 'native-
base';
import PropTypes from 'prop-types';

class Register extends React.Component {
  state = {
    email: null,
    repeatEmail: null,
    name: null,
    password: null,
    address: null,
    postcode: null,
    city: null,
  };

  render() {
    return (
      <View style={{ flex: 1 }}>
        <Content>
          <Form>
            <Item>
              <Input
                placeholder="e-mail"
                keyboardType={'email-address'}
                autoCapitalize={'none'}
                onChangeText={email => this.setState({ email })}
              />
```

```
    </Item>
    <Item>
      <Input
        placeholder="repeat e-mail"
        autoCapitalize={'none'}
        keyboardType={'email-address'}
        onChangeText={repeatEmail => this.setState({
                                      repeatEmail })}
      />
    </Item>
    <Item>
      <Input
        placeholder="name"
        onChangeText={name => this.setState({ name })}
      />
    </Item>
    <Item>
      <Input
        placeholder="password"
        secureTextEntry
        onChangeText={password => this.setState({ password })}
      />
    </Item>
    <Item>
      <Input
        placeholder="address"
        onChangeText={address => this.setState({ address })}
      />
    </Item>
    <Item>
      <Input
        placeholder="postcode"
        onChangeText={postcode => this.setState({ postcode })}
      />
    </Item>
    <Item>
      <Input
        placeholder="city"
        onChangeText={city => this.setState({ city })}
      />
    </Item>
    <Button
      block
      style={{ margin: 20 }}
      onPress={() =>
        this.props.register({
          email: this.state.email,
          repeatEmail: this.state.repeatEmail,
```

```
                            name: this.state.name,
                            password: this.state.password,
                            address: this.state.address,
                            postcode: this.state.postcode,
                            city: this.state.city,
                         })}
                  >
                      <Text>Register</Text>
                  </Button>
              </Form>
              <LinkButton
                  title={'or Login'}
                  onPress={() => this.props.changeToLogin()}
              />
              {this.props.loading && <Spinner />}
            </Content>
            {this.props.error && (
              <Text
                  style={{
                      alignSelf: 'center',
                      color: 'red',
                      position: 'absolute',
                      bottom: 10,
                  }}
              >
                  {this.props.error}
              </Text>
            )}
          </View>
        );
    }
}

Register.propTypes = {
    register: PropTypes.func.isRequired,
    changeToLogin: PropTypes.func.isRequired,
    error: PropTypes.string,
    loading: PropTypes.bool,
};

export default Register;
```

In this case, <LinkButton /> at the bottom of the view will invoke this.props.changeToLogin() when pressed to switch to the login view.

Sales

We added one last screen to demonstrate how different journeys can be linked together reusing screens and components. In this case, we will create a list of products with their prices reduced, which can be added directly to the cart for a quick purchase:

```
/*** src/screens/Sales.js ***/

import React from 'react';
import { ScrollView, Image } from 'react-native';

import { bindActionCreators } from 'redux';
import { connect } from 'react-redux';
import PropTypes from 'prop-types';

import {
  Icon,
  Card,
  CardItem,
  Left,
  Body,
  Text,
  Button,
  Right,
  Title,
} from 'native-base';
import * as ProductActions from '../reducers/products';

class Sales extends React.Component {
  static navigationOptions = {
    drawerLabel: 'Sales',
    tabBarIcon: () => <Icon name="home" />,
  };

  onBuyPress(product) {
    this.props.addProductToCart(product);
    setTimeout(() => this.props.navigation.navigate
    ('MyCart', { product }), 0);
  }

  render() {
    return (
      <ScrollView style={{ padding: 20 }}>
        {this.props.products.filter(p => p.discount).map(product => (
          <Card key={product.id}>
            <CardItem>
```

```
            <Left>
              <Body>
                <Text>{product.name}</Text>
                <Text note>{product.author}</Text>
              </Body>
            </Left>
          </CardItem>
          <CardItem cardBody>
            <Image
              source={{ uri: product.img }}
              style={{ height: 200, width: null, flex: 1 }}
            />
          </CardItem>
          <CardItem>
            <Left>
              <Title>${product.price}</Title>
            </Left>
            <Body>
              <Button transparent onPress={() =>
               this.onBuyPress(product)}>
                <Text>Add to cart</Text>
              </Button>
            </Body>
            <Right>
              <Text style={{ color: 'red' }}>
                {product.discount} off!</Text>
            </Right>
          </CardItem>
        </Card>
      )))}
    </ScrollView>
  );
  }
}

Sales.propTypes = {
  products: PropTypes.array.isRequired,
  addProductToCart: PropTypes.func.isRequired,
  navigation: PropTypes.any.isRequired,
};

function mapStateToProps(state) {
  return {
    products: state.productsReducer.products || [],
  };
}
function mapStateActionsToProps(dispatch) {
  return bindActionCreators(ProductActions, dispatch);
```

```
    }

    export default connect(mapStateToProps, mapStateActionsToProps)(Sales);
```

We will use the same full list of available products, already stored in Redux's state, to filter (by reduced price) and map into an appealing list item that are ready to be added to the cart by triggering the `onBuyPress()` method, which in turn triggers `addProductToCart()`:

```
    onBuyPress(product) {
        this.props.addProductToCart(product);
        setTimeout(() => this.props.navigation.navigate('MyCart',
                                            { product }), 0);
    }
```

Besides triggering this Redux action, `onBuyPress()` navigates to the `MyCart` screen, but it does so after the call stack is cleared to ensure the product has been added to the cart correctly.

At this stage, the purchase journey will kick in again allowing the user to log in (if not logged in yet), pay for the items, and confirm the purchase.

Summary

In this chapter, we developed several common functionalities present in most e-commerce apps, such as user login and registration, retrieving data from an API, purchase journeys, and payments.

We tied all the screens with a common app state managed through Redux, which makes this app scalable and easily maintainable.

With maintainability in mind, we added properties validation for all our components and screens. Moreover, we enforced standard code formatting and linting, using ESLint, so that the app is ready for various team members to align and develop comfortable new features or maintain the current ones.

Finally, we also added API mocking for the developers to work locally without needing a backend when building the mobile app.

Index